© Mark Reid 1⁹
First Edition Marcl
(first published by Ashridε
Second Edition Augι
Reprinted Novembє
Third Edition May

A catalogue record for this book is available from the British Library. British Library Cataloguing in Publication Data.

All maps within this publication are reproduced from the 1997 Ordnance Survey 1:25 000 Outdoor Leisure map with the permission of the Controller of Her Majesty's Stationery Office © Crown Copyright, Licence No.MC83224M.

Front cover photograph: 'Yorkshire Meadows, Gunnerside, Swaledale' © Dalescapes Photography by David Green, Hebden, North Yorkshire. Illustrations © John A. Ives, Dringhouses, York, YO24 1NB.

The contents of this publication are believed correct at time of copyright. Netherthless the author can not accept responsibility for errors and omissions, or for changes in details given. The information contained within this publication is intended only as a general guide. Walking and outdoor activities can be strenuous and individuals must ensure that they have suitable clothing, footwear, provisions, maps and are suitably fit before starting the walk; inexperienced walkers should be supervised.

'The Inn Way' is a registered trademark of Mark Reid

Published by:
INNWAY PUBLICATIONS
P.O. BOX 5975
BIRMINGHAM
B29 7EZ
ISBN 1 902001 03 6

Thank you to Bernadette, Stewart and Simon Reid, Paul
Stokes, Peter and Susan Hughes, Matthew Hunt, Carole
Rangeley, Anne and Judy Shepherd for being my walking
companions over the last two years.
Thank you to Bernadette Reid, Chris Bates and Michael
Freeman who assisted with proof reading.

I gratefully acknowledge the permission given by the authors
and publishers of the books used for quotations throughout
this publication. Every effort has been made to trace the
copyright holders for these short quotations. Unfortunately in
some instances I have been unable to do so and would
therefore be grateful for any information that may assist me
in contacting these copyright holders. Full credits to author
and title have been given in the text as well as in the
comprehensive bibliography at the back of this book.

Other books in this series:

The Inn Way ...to the English Lake District
by Mark Reid (ISBN 1 902001 01 X)

The Inn Way ...to Black Sheep Pubs
by Mark Reid (ISBN 1 902001 02 8)

www.innway.co.uk

The Inn Way
...to the Yorkshire Dales

**The complete and unique guide
to a circular walk in the
Yorkshire Dales.**

◆

The Inn Way ...to the Yorkshire Dales is a 76 mile
circular walk divided into six stages. Detailed maps,
route descriptions, fascinating historical quotes, snippets
and pieces of information will help guide you through
eleven of the most beautiful valleys in the world,
passing no less than 26 traditional English pubs and
leaving you with a deeper knowledge and
understanding of the Yorkshire Dales.

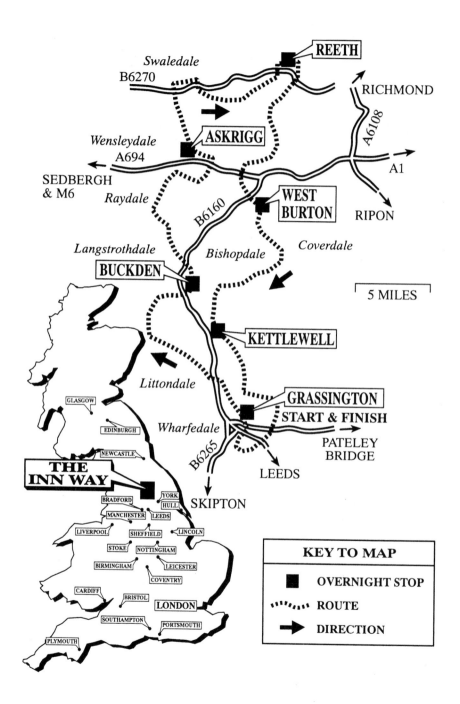

Swaledale
B6270

REETH

RICHMOND

A6108

ASKRIGG

Wensleydale
A694

SEDBERGH
& M6

Raydale

A1

**WEST
BURTON**

RIPON

Langstrothdale

Bishopdale

Coverdale

BUCKDEN

5 MILES

KETTLEWELL

Littondale

GRASSINGTON
START & FINISH

Wharfedale

PATELEY
BRIDGE

B6265

LEEDS

GLASGOW

EDINBURGH

NEWCASTLE

**THE
INN WAY**

YORK

HULL

SKIPTON

BRADFORD

MANCHESTER | LEEDS

LIVERPOOL

SHEFFIELD

LINCOLN

STOKE

NOTTINGHAM

BIRMINGHAM

LEICESTER

COVENTRY

CARDIFF

BRISTOL

LONDON

SOUTHAMPTON

PORTSMOUTH

PLYMOUTH

KEY TO MAP

■ **OVERNIGHT STOP**

░░░ **ROUTE**

➤ **DIRECTION**

4

A FOREWORD BY LUKE CASEY

Writer and presenter of Yorkshire/Tyne-Tees Television's
'The Dales Diary'.

I have read this latest edition of Mark Reid's excellent book with admiration and gratitude. Admiration for the way he has so thoughtfully combined fascinating fact with a superb guide which, by including twenty six thirst-slaking country inns, treats walkers as human beings rather than automatons in boots. And gratitude because now I have a volume I can lend to energetic friends without the fear that they'll be disappointed.

People who have never done it before but would love to have a go often ask me to suggest a nice Dales walk. After years of exploring the hidden treasures of this unique and beautiful part of the world, such a request, you would imagine, ought not to pose too much of a problem for me. But it always does. The reason is that when you send someone on their very first venture into your beloved hill country you want it to be a special experience for them. If only you could wave a magic wand and make the route you recommend yield up a lifetime of delights all in one go. Dales trekkers who share this love of the place will recognise the special moments:

Walking across a heather moor with a haze of pollen rising above an undulating sea of purple;

Watching the constantly shifting light unveil swathe after swathe of brilliant green on distant hills;

Listening to the chorus of hidden wild things telling their world that all is well;

Feeling, in that exquisite moment, part of it all and close to something greater than the squalid world of greed and inhumanity.

Of course, in my heart of hearts, I know there really is no need for magic wands. If music has charms to soothe the savage breast, the Dales have charms to seduce the sympathetic traveller. Time after time, confounding my fears, friends return from a recommended walk exuding contentment and peace. There is no need to ask if the hills have spoken to them. I can see it in their eyes.

Cheers to Mark Reid and The Inn Way for bringing a smile to mine.

CONTENTS

THE INN WAY

"Give me a map to look at, and I am content. Give me a map of country I know, and I am comforted: I live my travels over again; step by step, I recall the journeys I have made; half-forgotten incidents spring vividly to mind, and again I can suffer and rejoice at experiences which are once more made very real. Old maps are old friends, understood only by the man with whom they have travelled the miles. Nobody could read my maps as I do. Lend a book to a friend and he can enjoy it and miss nothing of its story: lend him a map, and he cannot even begin to read the tale it has to tell. For maps are personal things which books are not. The appeal of an old map is to the memory; an old map spread across my knees closes my eyes. The older, the more tattered it is, the greater my affection for it. I recall our adventures together in a storm and sunshine; an occasion, perhaps, when it slipped from my pocket and I searched my tracks anxiously, as for a lost companion, until it was found; an occasion, perhaps, when the mist was thick and instinct and the map urged different ways, and I followed the map and came to safe ground again. Ah yes, maps are grand companions. I have thrown books away, but never a map.

Give me a map of country I do not know, even of country I shall never know, and it has the power to thrill and excite me. No book has such an appeal to the imagination. A new map means new routes to plan, and ever so carefully, as the ground is strange and regard must be given to contours and watersheds and passes. My map becomes not a square of coloured linen, but a picture of the country itself. That blue daub becomes a glittering lake fringed by pine woods; the black specks a clustered village set amongst rich meadows in a corner of a valley; the faint red lines a steep mountain face soaring majestically into the heavens. My route is planned to the last detail, altered again and again; it is an ambitious programme, for there are no ties of home to bind me and limit the objective; expense is nothing. It is finished; it is perfect. It doesn't matter that I will never be able to do it. My pleasure has been great, yet, sadly enough, it is a pleasure shared by the very few. Map-lovers are scarce, book-lovers many, yet I think the reward of the lover of maps is far and away the greater. If it is ever my lot to be cast away on a desert island, let it be with an atlas and a one-inch map of the Lake District."

A.Wainwright,
'A Pennine Journey - The Story of a Long Walk in 1938'.

INTRODUCTION

I grew up in the spa town of Harrogate, which is situated on the lower eastern flanks of the Pennines, and I have many fond childhood memories of the Dales; nervously walking behind Hardraw Force whilst clinging to the rock face, paddling in the Ure at Aysgarth and scrambling amongst the rocks at Brimham. But I can clearly remember the moment when I fell in love with the Dales. It was a warm Saturday afternoon in May 1985 and my parents drove me from Harrogate to Reeth to perform in my school band as part of the Swaledale Festival that evening. The other band members had travelled earlier in the day but unfortunately I had to revise for my fast approaching 'O' Levels. It was as we crossed Bellerby Moor and started to drop down towards Swaledale that my mother pulled the car off the unfenced road to admire the view. I got out of the car and stood there completely captivated by what I saw; the heather clad moorland swept down to the valley of the Swale, and way in the distance Reeth stood proudly on the flanks of Calver Hill, bathed in golden sunshine. I was filled with a sense of well being. From that day I have visited every part of the Dales, read and collected as many books as possible and spent many happy holidays there. I was fortunate enough to study Geography at Lancaster University, which has given me a deeper understanding of the physical and human geography of the area. After graduating I started my career with Tetley's Brewery in Leeds where I was given an area to look after for six months as part of my training - I looked after all freehouses between Kettlewell and Hebden Bridge.

The idea of The Inn Way is to put this knowledge and love of the Dales into a walk so that people who wish to discover the Dales may do so with the assurance that they are seeing and experiencing the best the area has to offer. I marked on a map my favourite places including villages, viewpoints, castles, bridges and pubs and then joined them up to form a circular walk. The walk starts and finishes in Grassington, which is easily accessible and offers ample facilities and services, and will take six days to complete covering 76 miles. Eleven Dales and twenty six inns are passed along the way (which serve ales from at least ten different breweries), as well as Roman roads and forts, haunted bridges and the corpse way, a medieval castle which held Mary Queen of Scots, Brigantes dikes, monastic roads and guideposts, nature reserves, waterfalls, lead mines, glacial lakes, breathtaking views and much, much more. The six stages are designed so they are between eleven and fourteen miles in length, and that you pass at least one pub at lunchtime and the overnight village has plenty of facilities.

LINTON CHURCH

PLAN OF THE BOOK

The Inn Way ...to the Yorkshire Dales will take six days to complete either as a 76 mile circular walk or broken down into individual linear walks of up to fourteen miles. This book is divided into six sections, each of which is designed to provide all of the necessary information for that day's walk. Every section contains an information page, route description, hand drawn map and a detailed compilation of information concerning places of interest illustrated with quotations from a very varied selection of travel authors who have visited the Dales over the last 100 years.

Interpretation of Information and Route Descriptions

Walk Information

Points of interest: These are a summary of the highlights of the day's walk.

Distance: The distance travelled in a day has been broken down into 'morning' and 'afternoon' sections with a total mileage. The distances given are 'map miles' estimated using Ordnance Survey maps (1:25000). All distances given are in miles and yards.
Conversions are as follows,
Yards to metres mutiply by 0.9144
Miles to kilometres multiply by 1.6093
Metres to yards multiply by 1.0936
Kilometres to miles multiply by 0.6213

Time: Total time taken to complete the day's walk based upon a walking speed of three miles per hour with consideration for steep ascents, sightseeing and rest/food breaks.

Terrain:	Summary of the type of ground you will encounter for example mud, long grass, gravel as well as any particularly exposed sections, steep ascents/descents.
Ascent:	The first figure relates to the largest single climb of the day. The second figure is the maximum height gained. All height figures are in metres (see conversion table above).
Viewpoints:	The most spectacular viewpoints are listed for each section. Remember your camera.

Facilities:

Inn	See list of 'Public Houses'.
B&B	Bed and Breakfast available in the village.
Shop	At least one shop selling general provisions.
P.O.	Post Office, which may also sell limited provisions.
Cafe	Teas and light refreshments available
Bus	Bus service, although often infrequent and may vary seasonally.
Phone	Public payphone.
Toilets	Public toilets.
Information	Yorkshire Dales National Park Information Points offering local information.

Route Descriptions:

The abbreviations 'SP' for signpost, 'FP' for footpath, 'BW' for bridleway and 'FB' for footbridge have been used. The route has been walked several times using solely the descriptions given, however to ensure ease of use they should be used in conjunction with the maps. Each route description has been divided into paragraphs which correspond with one of the sixteen detailed maps. Public rights of way or permitted access areas may only be used during the completion of the walk; this walk only follows such routes. Occasionally rights of way may be altered to prevent erosion damage etc, these changes are clearly signposted and must be followed.

THE MAPS

Each one of the sixteen hand drawn maps are designed to tie in with the route descriptions. The route is easy to follow and is marked by a series of dots along footpaths and bridleways or arrows along roads and tracks (see 'Key to Maps'). Landmarks, places of interest, hills and contours are also given to help you. These maps should guide you safely around The Inn Way ...to the Yorkshire Dales, however they do not show the surrounding countryside in great detail. Should you require detailed information I recommend the following Ordnance Survey maps:-

Ordnance Survey Outdoor Leisure Map 1:25,000 Sheet 2 'Yorkshire Dales Southern & Western areas', showing lower Wharfedale from Kettlewell, lower Littondale and the environs of Grassington.

Ordnance Survey Outdoor Leisure Map 1:25,000 Sheet 30 'Yorkshire Dales Northern & Central areas', showing all of Swaledale, Wensleydale, Coverdale and Upper Wharfedale and Littondale.

Ordnance Survey Landranger 1:50,000 Sheet 98 Wensleydale & Upper Wharfedale- this covers the whole of the walk, but is less detailed.

KEY TO THE MAPS

ONE MILE (1 MILE = 1.61 KM)

CRAG OR SCAR

CONTOURS WITH HEIGHT
IN METRES

DECIDUOUS   CONIFEROUS
WOODLAND

B6270

ROAD (METALLED)
WITH DESTINATION   REETH

BUILDINGS   CHURCH

TRACK

RAILWAY LINE

RAILWAY LINE (DISUSED)

MAIDEN
CASTLE

EARTHWORKS

RIVER WITH
BRIDGE

607

CAIRN (HEIGHT IN METRES)

spr. -   SPRING

Y.H. -   YOUTH HOSTEL

V   -   OUTSTANDING
            VIEWPOINT

FB   -   FOOTBRIDGE

PUB -   SEE "PUBLIC HOUSES'

INN WAY ROUTE ALONG
TRACK / ROAD

INN WAY ROUTE ALONG
FOOTPATH / BRIDLEWAY

FACILITIES PROVIDED AT EACH OF THE STAGES

Stage One - Grassington

Grassington serves as the starting and finishing point for two main reasons - it is easy to get to and it offers ample facilities.

How to get there
By public transport - the nearest train station is at Skipton and relatively frequent bus services run between Skipton and Grassington.

By car - Skipton is reached via the A65 from Leeds, A650 from Bradford or the A59 from Harrogate to the east or Preston from the west. The B6265 heads north from Skipton directly to Grassington. There is a large 'pay and display' car park in the village that is run by the National Park Authority. Ask in the Information Centre about details of long stay parking.

Facilities
Grassington offers the following - B&B's, hotels, holiday cottages, craft shops, fruit shops, small supermarket, general stores, off licence, fish and chip shop, cafes, Barclays Bank (cashpoint), bus service, police station, restaurant, bookshop, folk museum, garage, doctor's surgery, outdoor pursuits shop, telephones, toilets and three pubs. The National Park Information Centre has details on local events, services, facilities and accommodation. Maps, books and literature associated with the Dales are available. It houses a display area which provides a fascinating insight into the influences behind the geography, geology and landscape of the Dales and also illustrates how the park is managed to try to strike a balance between conservation, recreational use and the people who live and work in the Dales.

Stage Two - Buckden

Buckden offers B&B's, hotel, general store, tea room and restaurant, craft shops, outdoor recreation centre, holiday cottages, telephones, toilets, bus service, large car park, National Park Information Point, National Trust Interpretative Centre and the Buck Inn.

Stage Three - Askrigg

Askrigg offers B&B's, restaurant, post office and general stores, bus service, cafe, outdoor pursuits centre, village shop, craft shops, toilets, telephones and two pubs.

Stage Four - Reeth

Reeth offers several B&B's, hotels, youth hostel at Grinton, restaurant, tea rooms, Barclays Bank (no cashpoint), craft and gift shops, bakery, general stores, post office and bookshop, newsagent, garage, doctor's surgery, folk museum, National Park Information Centre, traveling fish & chip van (Fridays), toilets, telephones, bus service and three pubs.

Stage Five - West Burton

West Burton offers B&B's, post office, butcher, village store, craft shop, telephone, bus service and the Fox and Hounds.

Stage Six - Kettlewell

Kettlewell offers numerous B&B's, hotels, restaurant, general stores, post office, youth hostel, craft shop, tea rooms, garage, large car park, bus service, National Park Information Point, outdoor pursuits shop, toilets, telephones and three pubs.

All of the above information is for guide purposes only and many facilities are liable to change.

If it is important - check it.

USEFUL INFORMATION

InnWay Publications Website: http://www.innway.co.uk

Tourist Information Centres and National Park Centres:

Aysgarth Falls*	Telephone: 01969 663424
Grassington*	Telephone: 01756 752774
Harrogate	Telephone: 01423 537300
Hawes*	Telephone: 01969 667450
Leyburn	Telephone: 01969 623069
Reeth*	Telephone: 01748 884059
Richmond	Telephone: 01748 850252
Skipton	Telephone: 01756 792809

National Park Centres* offer in-depth local knowledge and interpretative displays of issues facing the area and Dales life in general through various forms of media. They also from a point of contact for the Ranger Service and weather information.

Yorkshire Tourist Board
Telephone: 01904 707961
312 Tadcaster Road
York
YO24 1GS
Yorkshire Tourist Board website: http://www.ytb.org.uk

Youth Hostels
Located at Grinton, Aysgarth Falls, Linton and Kettlewell.
Call Y.H.A. on 01727 855215 for information.

Yorkshire Dales National Park
Telephone: 01756 752748
Hebden Road
Grassington
North Yorkshire

Baggage Courier Service
Telephone: 01729 830463
J. M. Schofield
Kirkby Malham
BD23 4BX

National Express bookings
Telephone: 0990 808080

Rail enquiries
Telephone: 0345 484950

Bus Services *for information please call the following:*
MetroLine (West Yorkshire)
Telephone: 01132 457676
Keighley & District Travel
Telephone: 01535 603284
Harrogate & District Travel
Telephone: 01423 566061
United Automobile Services
Telephone: 01325 468771

For further information contact Skipton TIC

Campaign For Real Ale CAMRA
Telephone: 01727 867201
230 Hatfield Road
St Albans
Hertfordshire
AL1 4LW

SAFETY

· Obtain a detailed weather forecast before setting out on your walk. If the weather turns bad do not hesitate to turn back the way you have come, as weather conditions can change for the worse within a matter of minutes reducing visibility and making walking hazardous. The temperature, wind speed and general weather conditions on the fells can vary significantly from the conditions at valley level. Never underestimate the strenuous nature of walking, particularly when this is combined with high ground and the elements.

· Waterproof and windproof coat and trousers are essential as well as gloves, hat and fleece for warmth.

· Your boots are the most important thing - make sure that they are waterproof, comfortable and have good ankle support and sturdy soles.

· Travel light as a heavy rucksack can tire you out, cause backache and make your shoulders sore. Take only essential items such as change of clothes (remember that several thin layers will keep you warmer than thick bulky layers and take up less room), nourishing snack foods, basic first aid kit, blister plasters, sun cream, whistle, water bottle, torch and 'survival' bag. Line your rucksack with a large plastic bag or bin liner to keep the contents dry

· Take Ordnance Survey maps (1:25,000) of the area and a compass - and learn how to use it!

· Drink plenty of fluids (not alcohol) and eat food regularly to keep energy levels up.

· Always walk in a group unless you are very experienced and inform someone of your intended route and report your safe arrival. If you are delayed but safe then make sure you let someone know so that the Fell Rescue are not called out. Do not attempt to complete a walk that is beyond your skill, experience or level of fitness. In an emergency summon help with six blasts of your whistle or call the Fell Rescue by contacting the police giving details of the incident and location.

• Do not explore old mine or quarry workings.

REMEMBER:
"An experienced walker knows when to turn back"

John A. Ives

PUBLIC HOUSES

1. Black Horse Hotel, Garrs Lane, Grassington: 01756 752770
Set back from the cobbled square, this imposing whitewashed old coaching inn offers a warm welcome with open fires and a good range of real ales.
ACC/FOOD/GDN/FIRE/TRAD

2. Devonshire Hotel, Main Street, Grassington: 01756 752525
Beautiful old stone built coaching inn with separate lounge and dining room areas which are comfortably furnished to cater for the large numbers of visitors to the village.
ACC/FOOD/GDN/FIRE/TRAD

3. Foresters Arms, Main Street, Grassington: 01756 752349
Set in the heart of Grassington this pub is the village 'local'; the pub has been run by the same family for over 25 years. Separate rooms and a games room ensure that this pub is full of atmosphere and is a popular meeting place. It also serves an excellent pint of beer.
ACC/FOOD/GDN/FIRE/TRAD/BAR

4. Tennant Arms, Kilnsey: 01756 752301
This 17th century coaching inn has a spectacular setting with Kilnsey Crag dominating the scene.
ACC/FOOD/GDN/TRAD/FIRE/BAR

5. Falcon Inn, Arncliffe: 01756 770205
When you walk into this pub you step back in time; wooden bench seating, several small rooms, outside loos and beer straight from the cask. A visit to this beautiful old hostelry is a must.
ACC/FOOD/GDN/TRAD/FIRE/BAR

6. Queens Arms, Litton: 01756 770208
Lovely old Dales pub with oak beams, flagged floors and open fires. Beautiful setting at the foot of Old Cote Moor and Horse Head Moor, with unsurpassed views across the valley and up towards the dale-head.
ACC/FOOD/GDN/TRAD/FIRE/BAR

7. Buck Inn, Buckden: 01756 760228

This imposing building in the heart of the village operates as a busy hotel, restaurant and pub. The small stone flagged bar area retains a great deal of character with open fires and a good range of real ales on offer. Superb views across Wharfedale from the benches at the front of this stone inn.

ACC/FOOD/GDN/TRAD/FIRE/BAR

8. White Lion, Cray: 01756 760262

There is not much to Cray, a farm or two and the pub, but its setting amongst waterfalls and the surrounding wild moorland is superb. The tiny White Lion offers open fires, stone flagged floors, beamed ceilings and excellent ale to compensate for the often bleak weather outside.

ACC/FOOD/GDN/TRAD/FIRE/BAR

9. Rose and Crown, Bainbridge: 01969 650225

This pub dates back to 1445, although it was much altered in the 19th century, and has been providing hospitality for travellers for centuries. The Bainbridge Forest Horn hangs in the passageway; the horn was blown during the winter months to guide people through the forest of Wensleydale, a tradition which continues today.

ACC/FOOD/GDN/TRAD/FIRE/BAR

10. Victoria Arms, Worton: 01969 650314

Unassuming small pub situated along the main A684 but a closer look will reveal an unspoilt Dales local. This is one of the last surviving examples in England of a time when most landlords of country inns would also have a smallholding. The landlord keeps a flock of sheep as well as a good pint! The walls are full of fascinating bric-a-brac, but watch out for the back-end of the stuffed fox!

FOOD/TRAD/FIRE/BAR

11. King's Arms Hotel, Askrigg: 01969 650258

The King's Arms will be familiar to many people as the 'Drover's Arms' from BBC TV's 'All Creatures Great and Small'. The building dates from the 18th century and was originally a manor house but later developed into a coaching inn; Turner once stayed

here whilst painting in the Dales. Wood panelling, an inglenook fireplace and ancestral portraits help retain the manorial atmosphere.
ACC/FOOD/GDN/TRAD/FIRE/BAR

12. Crown Inn, Askrigg: 01969 650298
This unpretentious pub has a warm, friendly atmosphere and offers everything a traditional village local should. An old cast iron range warms one of the small snug areas, whilst locals play darts in another. Serves excellent homemade ham and pies.
FOOD/GDN/TRAD/FIRE/BAR

13. King's Head, Gunnerside: 01748 886261
Stone built pub close to the bridge over Gunnerside Gill. An open fire, stone floors, wholesome food and a genuine and friendly atmosphere make you want to stay all afternoon.
FOOD/GDN/TRAD/FIRE/BAR

14. The Black Bull, Reeth: 01748 884213
Ancient inn overlooking the green. The opened up bar retains a corner of great character with low beams and large fireplace; this was the scene from a Herriot film. Slanting corridors and low doorways add to the 'olde worlde' feel. Note the upside-down pub sign, the result of a long running dispute with the National Park over planning regulations.
ACC/FOOD/GDN/TRAD/FIRE/BAR

15. King's Arms, Reeth: 01748 884259
This impressive Georgian building is known locally as the Middle House. The bar is comfortable with a lively, local atmosphere and is warmed by a huge inglenook fireplace.
ACC/FOOD/GDN/TRAD/FIRE

16. Buck Hotel, Reeth: 01748 884210
Situated at the junction of the Swaledale and Arkengarthdale roads, the Buck offers a comfortable spacious interior catering for the many visitors to Reeth.
ACC/FOOD/GDN/TRAD/FIRE

17. Bridge Hotel, Grinton: 01748 884224

This stone built inn is aptly named for it is situated between Grinton Bridge and the smaller bridge over Grinton Gill. The interior is divided into several rooms on various levels warmed by open fires.
ACC/FOOD/GDN/TRAD/FIRE

18. Wheatsheaf Hotel, Carperby: 01969 663216

Several small rooms help create a cosy atmosphere; the real life James Herriot had his honeymoon break here in the 1940's, and Greta Garbo and Henry Hall stayed here in 1942.
ACC/FOOD/GDN/TRAD/FIRE

19. Palmer Flatt Hotel, Aysgarth Falls: 01969 663228

Situated above the falls on the A684 Leyburn to Hawes road. The hotel stands on the site of a hospice for pilgrims returning from the Holy Land in the time of the Crusades, hence the unusual name. The interior is spacious and furnished in a traditional style to cater for the overwhelming number of visitors to the falls during the summer months.
ACC/FOOD/GDN/TRAD/FIRE

20. Fox and Hounds, West Burton: 01969 663279

A lovely small inn offering excellent local ales in a comfortable bar with extensive views over the spacious village green; probably the best beer garden in the world!
ACC/FOOD/GDN/TRAD/FIRE

21 Thwaite Arms, Horsehouse: 01969 640206

A classic stone built Dales pub with a cobbled and flagged forecourt, several small rooms inside with stone flagged floors, bench seating and open fires. One of the remotest pubs in the country, but well worth the visit. Phone to confirm lunchtime opening times.
ACC/FOOD/GDN/TRAD/FIRE/BAR

22. King's Head, Kettlewell: 01756 760242

Tucked away in the heart of the village, this pub attracts a mixture of locals and visitors. A pub of great character with a superb inglenook fireplace dominating the bar and a superb range of excellent Real Ales.
ACC/FOOD/GDN/TRAD/FIRE/BAR

23. *Blue Bell Hotel, Kettlewell: 01756 760230*

Attractive whitewashed inn dating back to 1680 situated on the main B6160 through the village. Opened up interior retains a traditional bar area warmed by a roaring fire. Note the impressive selection of malt whiskies on sale.
ACC/FOOD/GDN/TRAD/FIRE/BAR

24 *Racehorses Hotel, Kettlewell: 01756 760233*

Large hotel situated directly opposite the Blue Bell and backing onto the River Wharfe. The comfortable interior is divided into several rooms with some lovely old stone fireplaces.
ACC/FOOD/GDN/TRAD/FIRE

25. *Clarendon Hotel, Hebden: 01756 752446*

Large Victorian stone built pub on the main Grassington to Pateley Bridge road. Lively unpretentious village local offering excellent Timothy Taylor's beers.
ACC/FOOD/GDN/TRAD/FIRE

26. *Fountaine Inn, Linton: 01756 752210*

Beautiful old whitewashed inn overlooking the delightful village green and beck. The interior retains the character of an old fashioned Dales pub with small rooms, low ceilings, open fires and bench seating.
FOOD/GDN/TRAD/FIRE/BAR

KEY
. . . .

ACC	Accommodation
FOOD	Meals available
FIRE	Open fires
GDN	Beer garden (includes lawns, patios and outside benches)
TRAD	Cask ales available (Real Ale)
BAR	Traditional public bar area often with flagged floor.

THE BREWERIES

The following breweries supply outlets in the Dales. The vast majority of pubs and inns in this area are free houses and therefore the landlord is able to stock whichever brand of beer he/she likes. You may find beers on sale which are not listed below; if you do then have fun sampling them !

NATIONAL BREWERS

SCOTTISH COURAGE LTD

Scottish Courage Ltd is the new beer division of Scottish and Newcastle plc which was formed following the merger of Scottish and Newcastle Breweries and Courage Ltd in 1995. This follows a previous 'pubs for breweries' swap in 1991 between Grand Metropolitan and Courage giving the brewing side to Courage. The result is the largest brewing company in the country with an emphasis on the free trade market. The full portfolio of breweries and ales which make up this company have not been listed, only the ones you will most likely find in the Dales area.

T & R Theakston Ltd,
Wellgarth, Masham, Ripon, North Yorkshire.
Established in 1827 in the small Dales market town of Masham, T & R Theakston Ltd. brew traditional cask conditioned ales. The Masham Brewery has an excellent visitors centre and a working cooper's shop, where one of the remaining eight brewery coopers in the country is employed, making wooden casks for local beer deliveries. The legendary Theakston Old Peculier is perhaps the most well known of the Theakston ales, in a portfolio which includes Best Bitter, XB, Black Bull and traditional Mild, together with a number of special occasional ales which are well worth looking out for. Once a small country brewer with a handful of pubs,

Theakston's ales are now available nationally making Theakston's a name synonymous with Real Ale. The production from the Masham Brewery is reserved for the Dales area, and to cope with demand the rest of the UK is supplied by Scottish-Courage's brewery at Newcastle Upon Tyne, although Old Peculier is only brewed at Masham.

Cask ales available include Mild (ABV 3.5%); Best Bitter (ABV 3.8%); Black Bull Bitter (ABV 3.9%); XB (ABV 4.5%); Old Peculier (ABV 5.6%).

Younger's Brewery
Fountain Brewery, 159 Fountainbridge, Edinburgh.

The cask ales produced at Edinburgh are sold throughout the North of England although Theakston's ales are taking their place on the bar more and more. Scotch bitters are particularly popular in the North East of England and they are characterised by a sweet taste.

Cask ale available Younger's Scotch Bitter (ABV 3.7%).

John Smiths's
Tadcaster, North Yorkshire

Established in 1758, John Smith's is the home of three traditional Yorkshire beers. The excellent John Smith's Yorkshire Bitter is now Britain's leading bitter brand. One of the oldest brands brewed at Tadcaster is Magnet Ale, a firm favourite in the club land of the North East and Websters Yorkshire Bitter popular in South Yorkshire. Interestingly John Smith's brother, Samuel, also set up a brewery at Tadcaster, which continues today as an independent company.

Cask ales available include John Smith's Bitter (ABV 3.8%); Magnet (ABV 4%); Webster's Yorkshire Bitter (ABV 3.5%).

CARLSBERG -TETLEY

This company was formed in 1992 following the merger of Allied Breweries and Carlsberg and operates several large breweries throughout the U.K. and is technically only a brewing company. Their portfolio includes many famous brands such as Tetley Bitter, Ansells, Draught Burton Ale and Carlsberg Export.

Joshua Tetley & Sons Ltd,
The Brewery, Leeds, West Yorkshire

Tetley Bitter is the flagship bitter brand for Carlsburg Tetley and is now available nationally, complete with newly designed pump-clip. Joshua Tetley started brewing his famous beers in 1822 and the brewery stands as one of the largest producers of cask ale in the country with its own multi-million pound visitors centre along the banks of the River Aire. This bitter can be found more frequently in the southern part of the Dales due to its proximity to the Tetley heartland of West Yorkshire.

Cask ales available include Bitter (ABV 3.7%); Mild (ABV 3.2%)

INDEPENDENT BREWERS

Timothy Taylor & Co,
Knowle Spring Brewery, Keighley, West Yorkshire

Famous independent brewery offering a large range of award winning ales. Production is limited and therefore stockists are few and far between, so if you find a pub selling Timothy Taylor's beers make sure you sample some. Landlord Pale Ale is the jewel in the crown and is particularly thirst quenching after a long day walking - it is characterised by a very dry, bitter and fruity flavour which is distinctive of the Taylor's brews.

Cask ales available include Dark Mild (ABV 3.5%); Golden Best (ABV 3.5%); Porter (ABV 3.8%); Best Bitter (ABV 4%); Landlord (ABV 4.3%); Ram Tam (ABV 4.3%).

Black Sheep Brewery PLC,
Wellgarth, Masham, North Yorkshire.

This independent brewery was set up in 1992 by Paul Theakston following the take-over of his family firm by Scottish and Newcastle Breweries in 1989. The brewery is situated next door to the offices of T & R Theakston Ltd in the old Lightfoot Brewery maltings. Three excellent 'Yorkshire style' bitters are produced for the free trade market, which are full bodied with a dry, well hopped flavour. The brewery has a superb visitors centre which offers guided tours and there is also a shop, bar and bistro. Black Sheep ales are becoming increasingly available throughout North Yorkshire and beyond.

Cask ales available include Best Bitter (ABV 3.8%); Special Ale (ABV4.4%); Riggwelter Strong Ale (ABV 5.9%).

Dent Brewery
Cowgill, Dent, Cumbria

Small brewery set up in 1990 in the Yorkshire Dales, although Dentdale actually falls into Cumbria. These fine ales are brewed using Dales spring water in a brewery that was once a barn, producing over 40 barrels a week for their two tied houses and a large free trade market, which is supplied through their own distribution company called Flying Firkin. Cask ales available include Bitter (ABV 3.7%); Ramsbottom Strong Ale (ABV 4.5%); T'owd Tup (ABV 6%); Aviator (ABV 4%); Kamikaze (ABV 5%) plus a range of seasonal ales.

Moorhouse's Brewery Ltd,
Burnley, Lancashire.

Small independent brewery which supplies a limited number of outlets with distinctive good quality beers. Cask ales available include Premier Bitter (ABV 3.6%); Pendle Witches Brew (ABV 5%).

THE HISTORY OF THE DALES

It has taken 300 million years for the land forms of the Yorkshire Dales to take shape, yet less than 10,000 years for man to manipulate this landscape. The landscape, land use and settlement pattern we see today is the result of over 1000 years of varying influences. The first inhabitants of the Dales came after the retreat of the glaciers and subsequent warming of the climate, these were the Stone Age hunter - gatherers who lived in cave dwellings some 9000 years ago (e.g. Elbolton Cave at Thorpe). By around 1300 BC flint tools were replaced by metal and this heralded the onset of the Bronze Age, however it was not until around 100 BC that man really made an impact on the landscape with the use of iron implements. The people of this Iron Age period were groups of tribes, predominantly Brigantes, collectively known as Celts. They settled and cultivated the land, favoured the well drained limestone areas because of the wet climate, and they built forts and defensive ditches. The shapes of their dwellings, square fields, burial circles and mounds can still be seen, indeed over 200 prehistoric sites have been identified within the Dales area including the impressive Lea Green settlement above Grassington and Tor Dyke above Kettlewell; they lived in the Dales right through the Roman occupation.

The Romans came to Britain in AD 43 and had little trouble overcoming the Celtic tribes. They set up forts and towns linked together by straight roads and established a sophisticated social structure. They saw the Dales as an inhospitable land and left it to the native Celtic population, although they did exploit the mineral deposits in the area notably lead from Swaledale and Wharfedale. Forts were established around the Dales at Greta Bridge, Brough, Bowes, Ilkley and Elslack and these were connected by several roads which divided the area into a series of blocks. A fort was established in the very heart of the Dales at Bainbridge and this was continually manned from AD 80 to AD 400 with a garrison of 500 men. Traces of this fort can still be found on Brough Hill, and the route of a Roman road can be clearly seen cutting a straight course across the moors. The Roman occupation ended in AD 409, however the now integrated Romano-British people continued to live in this area much as they had done before the end of Roman rule for another two centuries.

The next wave of settlers were the Angles from northern Germany in the 7th century. They moved into the lower reaches of the Dales from the Vale of York and cleared woodland to make way for small farming communities. They brought with them a new language, culture and system of agriculture and the settlement pattern we see today was largely established by these Anglian farmers. Place names ending in '-ley', '-ton' and '-ham' indicate Anglian settlements. Danish settlers came next and in-filled between Anglian villages, their settlements are indicated by '-by' and '-thorpe'. The Norsemen came across from the east of Ireland in the tenth century and settled in the Lake District and the upper reaches of the Dales, particularly Swaledale above Gunnerside, Wensleydale above Bainbridge, Wharfedale above Buckden and Arkengarthdale. The landscape reminded them of their home back in Norway; hills, mountains and narrow valleys with sparse woodland. These Norse settlers did not like to live in communities preferring single homesteads which complemented their style of pastoral farming. Places such as Keld, Muker and Gunnerside would have started as single Norse farms only developing into sizeable communities when the lead mines were developed. They grazed their livestock in the valleys during spring and autumn then moved them to the upland pastures over the summer months, leaving the grass to grow in the valley for use as winter fodder. These areas of upland grazing were known as 'saetrs' which can be seen today in the place names of the upper Dales, for example Gunnerside, Marsett, Countersett. Another common name is

'Thwaite' which meant a clearing in woodland in old Norse, for example Yockenthwaite in Langstrothdale. There are few physical remains of this period although the Norse language still remains today in the form of the old Dales dialect with words such as dale, fell, beck, crag, gill, scar, tarn, mere and garth. So the settlement pattern we see today was largely in place by the tenth century following the colonisation of the area by Anglo-Saxons, Danes and Norsemen.

Following the Norman Conquest in 1066 large tracts of land in the Dales were set aside as hunting preserves for the Lords of Richmond, Middleham and Skipton castles. Villages on the forest edge were developed as foresters' villages, notably Buckden, Bainbridge and Healaugh and a form of conservation was given to the 'chases' so that deer, boar and otter were protected. Apart from the hunting forests the Norman influence on the landscape was limited - by far the greatest influencing factor on land use in the Dales was from the monasteries. Fountains Abbey was founded in 1132, Jervaulx in 1145 and smaller priories were established at Coverham, Bolton, Easby, Ellerton and Marrick. Vasts tracts of land were given to the monasteries by the Norman lords to ensure a safe passage to the next world. Fountains Abbey was by far the largest landowner with a million acres of grazing land throughout the North of England, and at the height of their power almost all of the area which now comes under the National Park was controlled by monasteries. They brought with them excellent farming and sheep breeding skills and successfully ran these large grazing lands through a series of granges which were farms and chapels combined (the name 'cote' indicates the site of a former grange). The grange which controlled the Craven district was at Kilnsey. A series of tracks were constructed which connected granges, abbeys and grazing lands. Many tracks remain today as green lanes, for example Mastiles Lane. They also drained marshy land, cleared woods and scrubland and built some of the earliest walls which were used mainly to keep unwanted animals out.

Following the Dissolution of the Monasteries and subsequent land ownership changes between 1537-40 improvements in farming techniques continued especially with the enclosure of crofts around villages and farms. Prosperity improved and thus followed a period of house building throughout the Dales from 1670 to 1750.

Almost all of the drystone walls and enclosures we see today were constructed after Acts of Parliament between 1780 and 1820 when common village land was enclosed into rectangular fields thus improving land management. The upland areas were enclosed during the middle of the 19th century. These fields were planned on paper and can be clearly identified by their straight lines across the hillside, earlier walls can be identified by their curving shapes. There are hundreds of miles of stone walls in the Dales, the construction of which was an enormous task; one waller could complete six metres of wall in a day. More recently lead mining in the 19th century has left a legacy of shafts, tunnels, spoil heaps and miners' cottages whilst tourism in the 20th century is having a profound effect on the Dales landscape with car parks, caravan sites and traffic jams. The Yorkshire Dales National Park was designated in 1954 with three main aims:

- Preserve and enhance the natural beauty of the area.
- Promote the provision of facilities for recreational activities and the study of nature within the National Park.
- Give full consideration to local interests as well as the social and economic needs of the people living and working within the Dales.

The Yorkshire Dales National Park Committee is responsible for the management of the Park offering advice and assistance to local people and visitors, as well as acting as a local planning authority. It must be stressed that the Yorkshire Dales National Park is neither national nor a park; 99% of the 680 square miles which make up the Park is privately owned. It is interesting to note that there are 18,000 people living within the Park and 8,000,000 people visit the Park annually.

THE GEOLOGY OF THE DALES

The Dales are famous for their beautiful and awe inspiring scenery such as Kilnsey Crag and Malham Cove, Brimham Rocks or Aysgarth Falls. When you stand and admire these 'wonders of nature' you are actually looking at the result of millions of years of geological processes. The geology of the Dales is extremely complex, however three distinct areas can be identified. The area centred around Ingleborough, Malham and Grassington is dominated by Great Scar Limestone with characteristic features such as limestone pavements, potholes, crags, scars and caves. To the north of this area are the Yoredale Series of rocks which are made up of layers of limestone, sandstone and shale sandwiched together. In many places the weaker shales and sandstones have become eroded exposing limestone ledges over which waterfalls cascade, this limestone can also be seen as rock terraces along the valley sides. To the south of the Great Scar Limestone the area is dominated by sandstones which are often weathered into weird and wonderful shapes.

300 million years ago a warm, shallow sea washed across what is now the Yorkshire Dales. This sea was teeming with marine life and as a result billions of tiny shells were deposited on the sea bed compressing together to form a thick layer of limestone. As this ancient sea advanced and retreated sand and mud deposits were laid down by rivers draining into the sea thus creating layers of sandstone, shale and limestone on top of the Great Scar Limestone. These three types of rock form the basis of the Dales scenery. These rocks have been folded, uplifted and fractured through the movement of the earth's crust over millions of years. The result of these movements are the mountains, peaks and hills of the Pennines, fault lines such as the Craven Fault and mineral deposits such as lead.

This landscape has been modified by the effects of ice and water, especially during the series of Ice Ages between one million BC and 10,000 BC. Ice and snow covered much of the Dales, although the centre of the English ice-sheet was over the Lakeland fells. Glaciers followed the line of existing valleys scouring the landscape and taking soil and rock along with it. Glaciated U-shaped valleys were formed with steep sides and flat valley floors, as opposed to the V-shaped river valleys. Soil and less resistant rock were stripped from the hills leaving exposed limestone rock strata, this can be seen today in the form of limestone pavements and scars; at Kilnsey the outcrop of Great Scar Limestone has been undercut by glacial erosion leaving an overhanging rockface. As the glaciers retreated with the warming of the climate, soil and rock was dropped. This can be seen in the form of moraines which are crescent shaped ridges of glacial boulder clay across the valley floor deposited by a melting glacier. Moraines often trapped meltwater forming small lakes, examples of which are Semerwater and Malham Tarn. Most of these glacial lakes have gone but their former sites are often the first to flood during rainy weather. The road between Grinton and Fremington in Swaledale follows the line of a moraine across the valley. Drumlins occur in the lower reaches of the Dales most frequently in Craven and Ribblesdale, and are small rounded 'egg shaped' mounds or hills of glacial boulder clay caused by retreating glaciers. Often huge pieces of rock weighing several tons were transported many miles by the glaciers, these are known as erratics, examples of which are the Norber Erratics near Austwick which are large boulders of Silurian slate resting on a limestone plateau. The meltwaters were responsible for the many dry valleys and gorges which can be found in the limestone country. These were formed by water flowing over the frozen ground eroding away rocks and soil thus creating valleys, however as the climate warmed the water went underground leaving the valley dry. Most spectacular of all would have been the waterfall over Malham Cove; with a drop of over 70m this would have dwarfed Niagara !

FAUNA AND FLORA

The soils which cover the underlying rock strata are directly formed from these rocks. Limestone areas are characterised by thin, well drained, calcium rich soils which support an abundant and diverse plant life. Grassland dominates the scene characterised by springy, bright green turf. Some of the original open woodland remains at Grass Wood (home to over 400 species of flowering plants) and along the limestone scars on the valley sides mainly made up of ash, willow, birch and hazel. The many sheltered crevices in the limestone rock support numerous rare plants including green speenwort, purple wild thyme, salad burnet, herb paris, angular soloman's seal and dog's mercury. The soils that overlie the sandstones are gritty, porous and low in nutrients whilst shales produce soils heavy in clay. Upland areas with underlying sandstone rocks lack calcium which assists with the decomposition of plant material, therefore there is a build up of decaying plant matter which in turn impedes drainage. This process has been on-going for over 7000 years and has created a water logged, acidic peat layer up to four metres thick, which supports only a handful of plant species notably cotton-grass. Heather, bracken and bilberry flourish where there is better drainage, this is often man-made to provide heather for grouse moors. It is where limestone, gritstone and shale are found together that the most varied flora can be seen (Wensleydale is one of the finest areas in the country for variety of plants). The soils of the valley floor are richer, mainly due to glacial deposits, and support hay meadows good examples of which can be found at Gunnerside in Swaledale. Deciduous woodland, predominantly oak, can be found in the lower reaches of the Dales.

The uplands are home to birds such as curlews, short-eared owls, oystercatchers, skylarks, kestrels, merlins, buzzards and grouse, while the meadowland of the valleys attract meadow pipits, house martins, swallows, pied and yellow wagtails. Along the riverbank you may spot herons, dippers, kingfishers, sandmartins or sandpipers. Woodpeckers, dunnocks, pheasant and nuthatches can be seen in woodland areas. The Dales are home to a wide variety of wild mammals including rabbits, stoats, weasels, voles, hedgehogs, deer, grey and red squirrels, otters and hares.

GRASSINGTON TO BUCKDEN

✦

"Oh, how can I put into words the joys of a walk over country such as this; the scenes that delight the eyes, the blessed peace of mind, the sheer exuberance which fills your soul as you tread the firm turf? This is something to be lived, not read about. On these breezy heights, a transformation is wondrously wrought within you. Your thoughts are simple, in tune with your surroundings; the complicated problems you brought with you from the town are soothed away. Up here, you are near to your Creator; you are conscious of the infinite; you gain new perspectives; thoughts run in new strange channels; there are stirrings in your soul which are quite beyond the power of my pen to describe. Something happens to you in the silent places which never could in the towns, and it is a good thing to sit awhile in a quiet spot and meditate. The hills have a power to soothe and heal which is their very own. No man has ever sat alone on the top of a hill and planned a murder or a robbery, and no man ever came down from the hills without feeling in some way refreshed, and the better for his experience".

A.Wainwright, 'A Pennine Journey -
The Story of a Long Walk in 1938'.

WALK INFORMATION

Points of interest: Iron age settlements, two nature reserves, monastic granges and roads, breathtaking limestone scenery, Norse and Anglian settlements, hunting forests and some beautiful old pubs.

Distance

Grassington to Arncliffe	7 miles
Arncliffe to Buckden	6 miles
Total	13 miles

Time   Allow 7 hours

Terrain   Majority of walk along relatively easy riverside paths and over meadowland (firm ground); climb from Litton to Buckden very strenuous over exposed moorland (often boggy).

Ascent   350 metres. Max. height 607m

Viewpoints Descent from Lea Green towards Conistone with views towards Kilnsey Crag. The climb over Old Cote Moor offers excellent views of Littondale and Upper Wharfedale.

FACILITIES

Grassington	Inn / B&B / Shop / P.O. / Cafe / Bus / Phone / Toilets / Info
Conistone	Phone
Kilnsey	Inn / B&B / Cafe / Bus / Info
Hawkswick	B&B / Cafe
Arncliffe	Inn / B&B / P.O. / Cafe / Bus / Phone
Litton	Inn / B&B / P.O. / Phone / Info
Buckden	Inn / B&B / Shop / P.O. / Cafe / Bus / Phone / Toilets / Info

ROUTE DESCRIPTION

(Map One)

From the cobbled market place walk up the Main Street which leads to the Town Hall. Turn left here along Chapel Street until you reach Town Head Farm. Follow the FP through the farmyard (SP 'Dalesway Conistone') bearing left round the farm buildings to reach a gate at the far end of the farmyard (SP). Head straight on along the clear path (ignore path down to the left) through several wall stiles/gaps. As you approach Grass Wood on your left the path picks up a clearer green lane, follow the left branch of this grassy track which heads along the top of a small limestone ridge keeping the wood and limestone pavement to your left for 1/2 mile. Ignore the green lane that heads off to the right and continue across the limestone pavement following the less defined path, then drop down to cross the stone wall on your left by way of a ladder stile next to a gate at the end of the woods. Cross the stile and follow the path immediately to the right which leads to a rocky ravine. Take care getting to the other side, where you follow the rocky track heading left along the side of the ravine. The waymarked path heads up to the right through bracken to run alongside a wall and joins a clear grassy track that leads to a gate; the track becomes a clearly visible green lane all the way to Conistone. When you reach the metalled road turn right into the village, then left along the road (SP 'Kilnsey, Kettlewell'). Cross over the bridge and take the path (SP 'Scar Laithe') on the right immediately after the bridge which comes out to the right of a barn directly below the Crag.

(Map Two)

Turn right along the road for 3/4 mile until you reach a fork in the road, take the left fork to Arncliffe. Follow the road for 1 mile passing two plantations, after a ruined barn on the right take the FP to Hawkswick on the right (SP). Bear left down across the field to a gate (SP), continue straight on to join a track and turn right down this track past the wooden house on your right to reach a gate after the house. Head through the gate and follow the grassy track down to Hawkswick Bridge. Head right over the bridge, and left through the village until you reach a footbridge over the river (SP 'Arncliffe'), cross the bridge and take the path to the right along the river bank and through meadows all the way to Arncliffe Church; turn left at the church to reach the village green. Head right across the green and out of the bottom right hand corner of the village along the road to Malham. Cross over the bridge and take the track straight ahead (SP 'Litton, Halton Gill').

(Map Three)

Follow the track until you reach a stile, cross over and follow the well marked path across the fields over stiles and through gates until you reach the National Nature Reserve of Scoska Wood, and again follow the well marked path through the Nature Reserve along the riverbank. After leaving the reserve the path continues across some fields to a gate which leads to a riverside walk and eventually to a farm track near some farm buildings. Turn right along the track and cross the ford, then follow the BW left into Litton. Take the BW, marked Buckden, to the right of the pub past the farm and follow the grassy walled track down over a footbridge and steeply up the side of the fell alongside the wall. Follow the clear stony track up the side of the hill passing through two gates and a large wall gap (no gate) after which the clear path turns left and follows the wall steeply again to the summit. Continue along the wall, through a gate and start the descent following the track which bears slightly to the right, then joins the tumbledown wall again before cutting through a wall gap which is clearly marked. The way, marked with posts and cairns, bears left down the side of the fell. Eventually you reach a track heading to the left, ignore this and drop down a bit further to reach another track signposted BW towards the wood. This well defined track snakes down to the road, where you turn right, pass over the bridge and into Buckden.

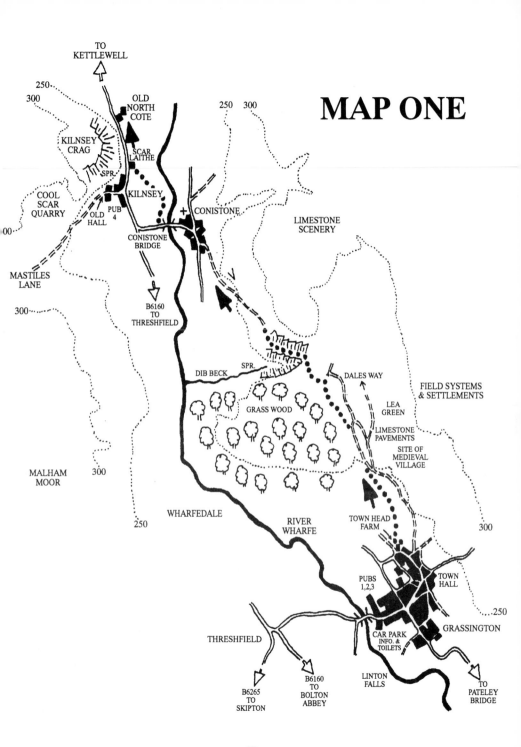

TO
KETTLEWELL

250
300

OLD
NORTH
COTE

KILNSEY
CRAG

SCAR
LAITHE

SPR.

COOL
SCAR
QUARRY

KILNSEY

00

OLD
HALL

PUB
4

250   300

MAP ONE

CONISTONE

LIMESTONE
SCENERY

MASTILES
LANE

CONISTONE
BRIDGE

300

B6160
TO
THRESHFIELD

DIB BECK   SPR.

DALES WAY

FIELD SYSTEMS
& SETTLEMENTS

GRASS WOOD

LEA
GREEN

LIMESTONE
PAVEMENTS

SITE OF
MEDIEVAL
VILLAGE

MALHAM
MOOR

300

WHARFEDALE

250

RIVER
WHARFE

TOWN HEAD
FARM

300

PUBS
1,2,3

TOWN
HALL

250

GRASSINGTON

THRESHFIELD

CAR PARK
INFO. &
TOILETS

B6265
TO
SKIPTON

B6160
TO
BOLTON
ABBEY

LINTON
FALLS

TO
PATELEY
BRIDGE

45

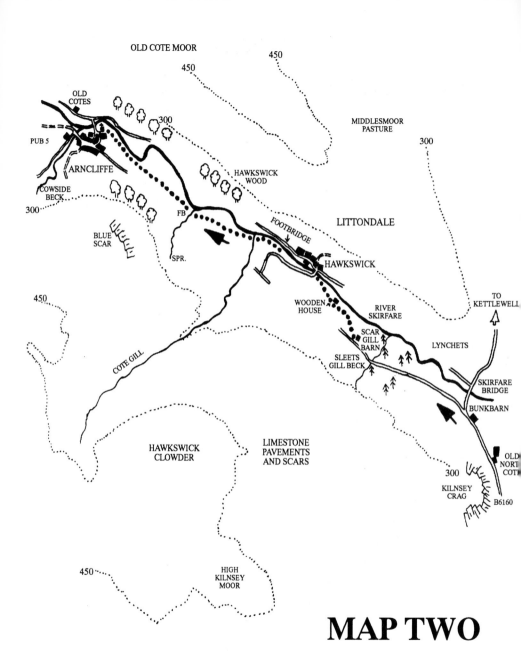

OLD COTE MOOR

450

450

OLD
COTES

300

MIDDLESMOOR
PASTURE

300

PUB 5

ARNCLIFFE

HAWKSWICK
WOOD

COWSIDE
BECK

300

FB

LITTONDALE

BLUE
SCAR

FOOTBRIDGE

SPR.

HAWKSWICK

450

WOODEN
HOUSE

RIVER
SKIRFARE

TO
KETTLEWELL

SCAR
GILL
BARN

LYNCHETS

SLEETS
GILL BECK

COTE GILL

SKIRFARE
BRIDGE

BUNKBARN

HAWKSWICK
CLOWDER

LIMESTONE
PAVEMENTS
AND SCARS

300

OLD
NORT
COT

450

HIGH
KILNSEY
MOOR

KILNSEY
CRAG

B6160

MAP TWO

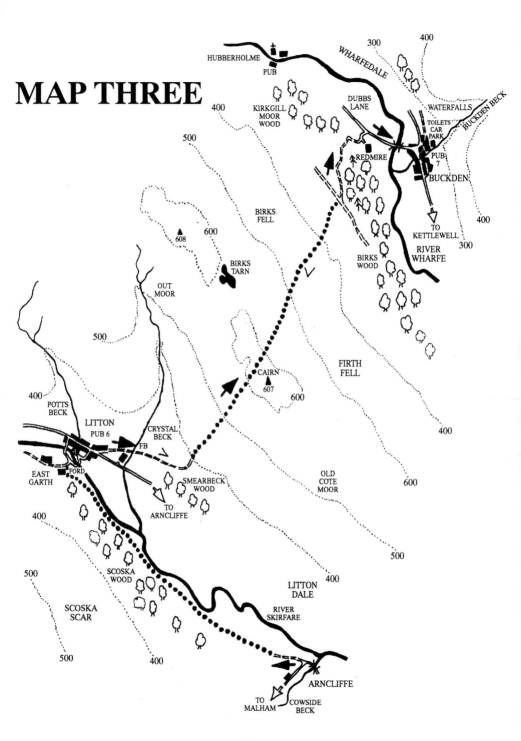

MAP THREE

HUBBERHOLME

WHARFEDALE

300

400

PUB

KIRKGILL
MOOR
WOOD

400

DUBBS
LANE

WATERFALLS

BUCKDEN BECK

TOILETS
CAR
PARK

REDMIRE

500

PUB
7

BUCKDEN

BIRKS
FELL

400

TO
KETTLEWELL

300

608

BIRKS
TARN

600

BIRKS
WOOD

RIVER
WHARFE

OUT
MOOR

500

CAIRN

607

FIRTH
FELL

600

400

POTTS
BECK

400

500

LITTON

PUB 6

CRYSTAL
BECK

600

FB

EAST
GARTH

FORD

SMEARBECK
WOOD

OLD
COTE
MOOR

600

400

TO
ARNCLIFFE

SCOSKA
WOOD

400

SCOSKA
SCAR

LITTON
DALE

500

RIVER
SKIRFARE

500

400

400

500

ARNCLIFFE

TO
MALHAM

COWSIDE
BECK

47

GRASSINGTON, pronounced 'Girston' locally, is the capital of Upper Wharfedale and home to over 1100 inhabitants. People have been living in this area for over 2000 years, originally at Lea Green and since the Norman times at Grassington. The Domesday Book of 1086 estimated the number of families living in the area to be twelve. After the Norman Conquest the manorial ownership passed from the Percys to the Plumptons, then to the Cliffords and finally to the Dukes of Devonshire. In the late 13th century Robert de Plumpton built the Old Hall as his hunting lodge, the building survives today as one of the oldest inhabited houses in England despite much modification in the 16th and 17th centuries. The Plumpton family had links with the monks of Fountains Abbey, indeed one reason for Grassington's growth is that it lies at the cross roads of two ancient roads - the monastic route from Fountains to the grazing areas of Kilnsey, and the road from Skipton to Richmond. It is believed that there is an underground passage which runs from the Old Hall to Hardy Grange, a house in Grassington which was once the property of Fountains Abbey. Grassington was granted a market charter in 1282, thus ensuring a rise in its importance within the local rural economy and the village soon developed as a trading centre in the forest of Wharfedale.

The real boom period was the 18th and 19th centuries when the Dukes of Devonshire developed the lead mines at Yarnbury on the moors above Grassington; many mining families moved to the area from Cornwall and Derbyshire and population levels were similar to those we see today. However, cheaper imports and dwindling reserves meant that by the 1880's mining had virtually ended. *"Although Grassington suffered greatly from the stoppage of the lead mines, it is now fast becoming popular as a health resort, and, as a native female quaintly remarked, 'We've gotten t' tellygraf; all 'at we're shot on nah is t' raelwey, an' then 'appen we'd keep ahr men at hoam."* (E.Bogg 'A Thousand Miles in Wharfedale' 1892).

The railway came to Threshfield in 1901 bringing new life to the area through tourism, however the passenger service ended in the 1930's although the line is still open to freight traffic serving the large and obtrusive Swinden Quarry near Linton. *"Grassington seemed a busy, thriving place as we came down to it from the hill settlement on a July afternoon. A farmer and his dog drove a flock of lambs and newly clipped sheep up the lane to the pastures. The frenzy of the coming haytime was in the air. Barns were cleared; sledges lay ready in the farmyards; and the cobbled streets resounded to the rattle of reapers on their way to the meadows. The clang of the anvil and the smell of burning horn came from the blacksmith's shop, and a newly shod horse clattered home ready for the strenuous work for the next few weeks."* (E.Pontefract & M.Hartley 'Wharfedale' 1938). Today Grassington is a popular tourist centre whose charm is not just the picturesque cobbled market place with its many interesting shops and old fashioned inns, but the hidden alleyways (folds) which lead off it. *"Wrinkled, winding alleys branch everywhere as the whim takes them. Pursuing these, you happen, when least expecting it, on a farmstead and the sweet breath of cattle."* (H.Sutcliffe 'The Striding Dales' 1929). The many folds were originally crofts running back from the main street, however over the years they have been filled in with houses. Buildings of interest include 'Theatre Cottage' off Garrs Lane, which was originally a barn where a theatre was housed in the early 19th century; Edmund Kean and Harriet Mellon appeared here in 1807. Pletts Barn is a fine example of a 17th century Dales barn, and it is reputed that Wesley once preached here. Town Head Farm dates from the 17th century and belongs to the Trustees of Fountaine Hospital in Linton, providing revenue for the Linton almshouses. On the main street is Tom Lee's Smiddy; In 1766 Lee murdered Dr Richard Petty after an argument at a Kilnsey hostelry and threw his body into the Wharfe. He was later hanged at York, and his gibbet irons are supposedly buried on the small mound near to Grassington Bridge.

LEA GREEN boasts one of the largest Iron Age settlements in England. It was occupied from around 200 BC to 400 AD, even during the Roman occupation, and comprises rectangular fields, hut circles and remnants of roads; nearby Celtic field systems of banks and terraces are reminders of this long forgotten community. *"The antiquity of this district is best proved by its earthworks and the remains of early Celtic days, which are to be seen just on the outskirts of the village to the north-west. These carry the mind back to a period when Druidical superstition prevailed in the forest, and the Roman eagle waved on the moorland."* (E.Bogg 1892).

GRASS WOOD is a beautiful piece (over 260 acres) of ancient woodland that once formed part of the much larger forest of Wharfedale. *"The Wharfe loves these woods and makes itself especially beautiful for them. A path on the right bank takes one through the meadows over stiles, then past quiet pools, rushes, falls and the Ghaistrills or spirit-holes, where the river hurrying into a narrow passage concentrates its full force till, set free, it rushes madly foaming into the next reach."* (C.Lewis 'Wharfedale'). It is a fascinating place with over 400 varieties of flowers, most of them exremely rare, and many archaeological remains thus meriting Nature Reserve status - a wonderful place to explore in spring. *"When you have known it a little time you have a personal feeling for the wood. It is alive, and entering it you feel welcomed or repelled as you would on meeting a person."* (E.Pontefract & M.Hartley 1938). Hidden away amongst the trees are the impressive stone ramparts and ditches of a Brigantes hill fort dating from AD70 known as Fort Gregory.

CONISTONE is a fine example of an Anglian settlement (8th century), with meadowland by the river, ploughing terraces (lynchets) on the slopes, common land on the fells and houses grouped around a green complete with maypole. Lynchets are indicative of a warmer climate many centuries ago as these ploughing terraces were once used to grow crops.

St Mary's Church has some fine pre-Norman arches and a wealth of interesting features including a poor box, despite 'restoration' in 1846. It is said to be the oldest building in Craven. In the churchyard is a sad memorial to a group of young men who were killed in a tragic pot-holing accident at Mossdale Cavern in 1967. *"If we could lift the curtain which hides the past, many a stirring scene and gathering of bygone people, peasant and monk, should we witness in and around this old kirkyard - the smile and gladness of a bridal party leaving the holy fane, or sounds of merrymaking greeting the ear - many a sign of tragedy throwing its shadow of human passion and errance on the mind-picture."* (E.Bogg 'By the Banks of the Wharfe' 1921). It is a beautiful but sleepy place with lovely old stone cottages and farms that seem to blend in perfectly with the surrounding limestone hills. Unfortunately there is no pub, *"...you can call for a cup of tea and a rest at the Post Office or at Mrs.Hill's, but remember nothing 'stronger' can be got in the way of liquid refreshment, as Conistone and Thorpe are the only villages in Upper Wharfedale without an inn."* (J.Crowther 'Rambles Round Grassington' 1920).

KILNSEY is dominated by its impressive crag; *"It is a natural phenomenon which reduces everything near it into insignificance. Its huge bulk jutting like a clenched fist into the valley dominates the middle dale."* (E.Pontefract & M.Hartley 1938). The crag is 170 feet high with an overhang of 40 feet that was undercut by the scouring action of glaciers thousands of years ago and now poses a challenge to rock climbers, *"...overhangs road and river as if threatening to crush whatever passes. Around this frowning rock all sorts of legends and fairy tales centre, and the village at its foot was once the abode of two witches who practised divination and sold charms."* (Fletcher 'Nooks and Corners of Yorkshire'). Clear, cool springs bubble up from the foot of the crag and it is said to be impossible to hit the crag with a stone thrown from the road.

The village of Kilnsey developed as a grange for Fountains Abbey in the 12th century, as the Abbey owned vast areas of grazing lands on the moors above Kilnsey. Mastiles Lane was originally a monastic drovers road which went to grazing lands in the Lake District; today it is a superb green lane. *"It (Kilnsey) has an ancient appearance, and only consists of some twelve houses, two of which are the 'Tenants Arms and the Anglers' Inn."* (J.Crowther 1920). The Anglers Arms, now closed, was where Dr Petty spent his last night before being murdered by Tom Lee in Grass Woods, a crime for which he was later hanged. Dr Petty's horse is said to haunt the woods. Behind the remaining inn stands the magnificent Kilnsey Old Hall which was built in 1648 on the site of the grange; Lady Anne Clifford used to stay at the Old Hall on her travels. Sadly the Hall has been neglected over the years and is now used as a barn; all that remains of the grange is part of the gatehouse.

LITTONDALE (originally called Amerdale), and the River Skirfare which runs through it (Skirfare means 'bright stream' in old Norse) make up some of the most beautiful scenery in England. *"Littondale is a pageant of loveliness all along its length and attains near perfection at Arncliffe."* (A.Wainwright 'In the Limestone Dales' 1991). Littondale is also steeped in history; there are traces of Iron Age settlements on the moors and the villages of today originally started life as Anglian settlements or Norse farmsteads. During Norman times the dale was a hunting forest, then the monks of Fountains Abbey used the limestone pastures for grazing as they once owned over 100 square miles land centred on Malham, Littondale and Wharfedale - a quick glance at the map will reveal many reminders of this once powerful landowner with names such as Monk's Road, Fountains Fell and many more still in use today. After the Dissolution of the Monastries the land continued to be farmed as it still is today - little has changed here for centuries. It is one of the few dales to have escaped lead mining, therefore the landscape and villages remain well preserved. Littondale is also noted for its variety of rare plants and flowers; the steep valley sides and limestone scars provide the ideal safe habitat for such flora. Littondale has many literary connections; Wordsworth mentioned it in his poem 'The White Doe of Rylstone', Charles Kingsley wrote about it in 'The Water Babies' and it was often used for locations in Emmerdale Farm.

HAWKSWICK (probably named after the birds of prey which once soared from the surrounding scars and crags) is a tiny farming hamlet. There is not much to do here except admire the beauty of the old limestone farmhouses and the views of the dale. *"In Hawkswick itself there is scarcely room by the river for houses; barn doors open towards the water's edge and one can sit and watch ducks from the breakfast table."* (N.Duerden 'Portrait of the Dales' 1978). The footpath alongside the River Skirfare between Hawkswick and Arncliffe is an absolute delight with river, meadows and steep valley sides creating a near-perfect scene.

ARNCLIFFE was originally an Anglian settlement whose layout has survived: a large village green around which houses huddle with crofts running back from the village. The name means 'eagle cliff'; the scars above Arncliffe would have been ideal nesting sites for birds of prey. There has been a church in Arncliffe since Saxon times, although the present church mainly dates from 1796 and 1841 when the Tudor church was pulled down and 'restoration' took place. The church tower survived and dates back to the 15th century. Inside the church there is a memorial to the local men who fought at the Battle of Flodden Field (1513); the church also has one of the oldest bells in the country, dated 1350, which was probably a gift from Fountains Abbey. *"The little river (Skirfare) is one of Yorkshire's most enchanting streams, and Arncliffe has an* *exquisite share of its valley, the village deep-set like a jewel between the wooded slopes of the moors and fells. The houses are round a green, and the Cowside Beck falls into the stream before it flows under a beautiful bow bridge and cascades by the churchyard. It would be hard to imagine a lovelier setting for the church, a simple place with a grey medieval tower peeping over a mantle of trees."* (A.Mee 'Yorkshire West Riding' 1941). It is a place of peace and tranquility, a place to pause and gather your thoughts.

The Falcon Inn is a superb Dales pub with wooden settles, open fires and beer straight from the cask, a living and integral part of our culture and heritage. *"The Falcon Inn stands as such a tavern should, unobtrusive in its simple dignity, instinct with the hospitality of other days."* (H.Sutcliffe 1929). There are some beautiful old stone barns which face onto the green; these barns were built at a time when crops were grown in the dale and were therefore designed with a porched doorway which allowed carts to be brought in under shelter, and rear doors which created a draft for threshing. Between Arncliffe and Litton lies Scoska Wood which is the largest ash and rowan wood left in the Dales, now protected as a nature reserve. The River Skirfare is also at its most playful in this area with the water disappearing beneath its bed of huge shelves of limestone rock, only reappearing again after heavy rain.

LITTON grew in importance as the fording point across the Skirfare of the old packhorse route to Settle; the monks of Fountains Abbey had a hospice here too. The Queens Arms has been refreshing travellers for over 150 years, I recommend you do the same before the arduous climb over to Buckden. *"The Buckden track joins the road by the house which has been an inn since 1842. The original inn, down a grassy lane between the road and the river, is now a barn....It was last kept by an old woman called Mrs Taylor. She avoided paying for a licence by selling penny or halfpenny parkins, and giving beer or ale with them. Now cows* *munch hay where her patrons ate parkin and drank 'free' beer."* (E.Pontefract & M.Hartley 1938). The view from the top of Old Cote Moor, between Litton and Buckden, is breathtaking, *"The outlook over Kettlewelldale from the edge of the moor at this spot is magnificent indeed; the rich green valley, with its river wandering dreamily, the villages reposing as in a charmed sleep in the embrasures of the eternal hills; and all the accessories of colour, light and shadow which are required to make a striking picture are found here."* (E.Bogg 1921).

BUCKDEN (meaning 'valley of the bucks') is the first, or last, village in Wharfedale and so has an air of importance about it. It grew in importance in Norman times when the area between Buckden and the dale head was a hunting forest known as Langstrothdale Chase, from the French 'Chasse' meaning 'hunting'. A mile to the south of the village stands Buckden Cross, which marked the limit of the old hunting forest, the preserve of the Earls of Northumberland. This forest was governed by its own laws, courts and privileges, and many of the forest officials would have lived here. The village once hosted two autumn fairs and supported three inns; now all that remains is the Buck Inn. *"In olden time Langstrothdale was one vast forest, and, in the memory of aged inhabitants, much more densely wooded than at present; the mountain slopes on the southern side of the stream are still well wooded. The dark green of the firs and the wild-looking glens present an appearance of weird grandeur truly Alpine."* (E.Bogg 1892).

Tourism has made more of an obvious impression at Buckden than most Dales villages, as the large car park and numerous holiday cottages testify, fortunately its setting amongst the fells can never be changed. *"...perched on the hillside like a Tibetan monastery..."* (A.Wainwright 'A Pennine Journey - The Story of a Long Walk in 1938' 1986). If you explore the many lanes that lead from the Buck Inn away from the main road you will discover the old 'heart' of Buckden with many lovely old cottages, farms, Wesleyan Chapel and village hall. Buckden Pike rises behind the village to a height of 702 metres (2302 feet). On the summit there is a memorial to the Polish crew of a RAF plane which crashed during bad weather in the Second World War. There was one survivor. He followed footprints in the snow of a fox, which eventually led him to a farm and safety. From the mid 17th century lead mining flourished on the flanks of Buckden Pike, centred on Buckden Beck, with mining activity continuing here until the late 19th century. Much of Upper Wharfedale, including Heber Farm, the the last working farm in Buckden, is now in the care of the National Trust who manage and protect over 6,100 acres of environmentally important and sensitive meadowland, ancient woodland and moorland. Buckden Rake, the stony path which leads towards Cray, is part of the Roman road which ran from Bainbridge to Ilkley. *"Buckden. So cradled is it in the heights that we seem to be inside a stupendous bowl as we stand where the farms and cottages and the ivied inn are gathered by the green."* (A.Mee 1941).

BUCKDEN TO ASKRIGG

✦

" There is only one way to know a hill, and that is to put your feet on it and walk. Wander about leisurely if you wish, but better still, make the summit your objective and struggle up to it. Plunge into the bracken and heather, and wrestle with the thousand tentacles that would hold you back; splash through the streams that silver the hillside; scramble up the rocks and know the thrill that enslaves the mountaineer; sweat and pant, slip and tumble, and curse if you are so minded, and rest often. But get to the top. And if up there you find a gale so strong as to bowl you off your feet, or you are privileged to be in the nerve-centre of a thunderstorm, so much the better. Stay on the summit as long as you may, then come down. Don't tread circumspectly now, but run; run as if all the fiends of hell were loose at your heels. Run with giant strides, leap, jump, tumble and sprawl and roll, come down helter-skelter until you reach the ground level in the valley. Wash in the stream, and bathe your wounds, and clean yourself up a bit. Then seek out a royal feed and a soft bed....If you have done all this, one of two things has happened to you. Either you will never want to see a hill again, in which case you may safely assume that the rot has settled in your soul so deeply that nothing will remove it; or you will hunger for the next opportunity, do it again and again, and keep young for ever."

A. Wainwright,
'A Pennine Journey - The Story of a Long Walk in 1938'.

WALK INFORMATION

Points of interest: Roman roads and forts, beautiful waterfalls, the legend of the flooded city, a forest village with its horn to guide travellers, fortified farmhouse, 'Skeldale House' as seen on TV and one of the finest 'green lane' walks in England.

Distance

Buckden to Bainbridge	9.5 miles
Bainbridge to Askrigg	3.5 miles
Total	13 miles

Time   Allow 6 hours

Terrain   Initial climb from Buckden to summit of Stake Moss is steep in places, though not as difficult as it first appears because the walk is along an excellent green lane/track with many flat stretches to catch your breath; the track over Stake Moss crosses exposed moorland. The remainder of the walk is along riverside paths and across meadowland.

Ascent   311 metres. Max. height 561 metres.

Viewpoints Buckden Rake looking across Langstrothdale.
Descent from Stake Moss towards Raydale.
View back towards Semerwater and out across Wensleydale from the path along the River Bain.

FACILITIES

Buckden	Inn / B&B / Shop / P.O. / Cafe / Bus / Phone / Toilets / Info
Cray	Inn
Stalling Busk	B&B / Phone
Bainbridge	Inn / B&B / Shop / P.O. / Bus / Phone / Toilets
Worton	Inn / B&B / Bus / Phone
Askrigg	Inn / B&B / Shop / P.O. / Cafe / Bus / Phone / Toilets / Info

ROUTE DESCRIPTION

(Map Four)

Leave Buckden car park using the gate at the top end (SP 'Cray High Bridge and Buckden Pike'), and follow the steep, stony path upwards. When the path levels out, bear left through the gate, observing the 'No Access' sign to the right, and continue straight ahead along the very clear 'green lane' all the way to Cray High Bridge and the metalled road (Note Cray down to your left). Turn right up along the road for 1/2 mile, as the road bears to the right take the well defined track to the left (SP 'Byway Stalling Busk'). Follow this track for 2 miles until you reach a second gate.

(Map Five)

Take the FP to the left of the gate (SP), and head straight on down hill along the clear grassy path over several wall stiles to reach a ruined barn. Cross the stile near to the barn and bear right to a stile to the left of a metal gate. Follow the grassy path over stiles and across Shaw Gate Gill until you reach the track again, and turn left. After 1/2 mile take the track down to the left which brings you out in Stalling Busk. Follow the road bearing right through the village past the 'phone box, and take the clear FP to the 'ruined church' bearing left ahead. At the church follow the SP to Semerwater to the right, which passes through a nature reserve and skirts the shore of Semerwater until it meets the metalled road. Turn left along the road, past the car parking area, to the bridge; take the FP to 'Bainbridge' to the right just before the bridge.

(Map Six)

Follow the path along the river bank (SP 'Bainbridge'), across a small wooden bridge, over a ladder stile and up the hill to a gate. Head straight on over 2 more stiles then follow the path as it skirts to the left round a small wooded ravine. The path meets a wall which you follow up to the right to a SP, then head left along the green lane towards Bainbridge. Just before you reach the road take the path between the road and the river which brings you out on the main road at the top end of Bainbridge. At the road go right to the T junction; the path continues through the wall stile ahead (SP 'Cubeck'). Follow the path up to the top of the wooded escarpment. At the top go left along a winding path which follows the escarpment and past Scar Top Farm and then through woodland until you reach a SP to 'Worton.' Drop down to the left through the wood, bear right across the fields (passing the end of the stone wall on your right) and head towards Worton. The path joins the road at the gate near to the farm buildings, turn right along the road then first left past the 'phone box, down over the bridge and bear round to the right to reach a FP to 'Aysgarth'. Follow the path along the river bank, over two footbridges to Nappa Mill. Turn left along the track until you reach a ford and a bridge to your left, take the stile directly ahead (SP) next to a gate. After the stile head towards the gate in the top right hand corner of the field, then straight on along the grassy track towards Nappa Hall. Go left along the farm track past the Hall to reach the road. Turn left along the road and take the FP to 'Askrigg' on the left just after the 'Nappa Scar' turning. Head down the bank and bear right across the field, over a stile and down across a beck then up the hill to another stile. Follow the clear path through six more wall gates to reach the road. Turn left along the Worton road, after the small bridge take the FP to the right through the farm yard. Follow this path over the hill directly into the centre of Askrigg.

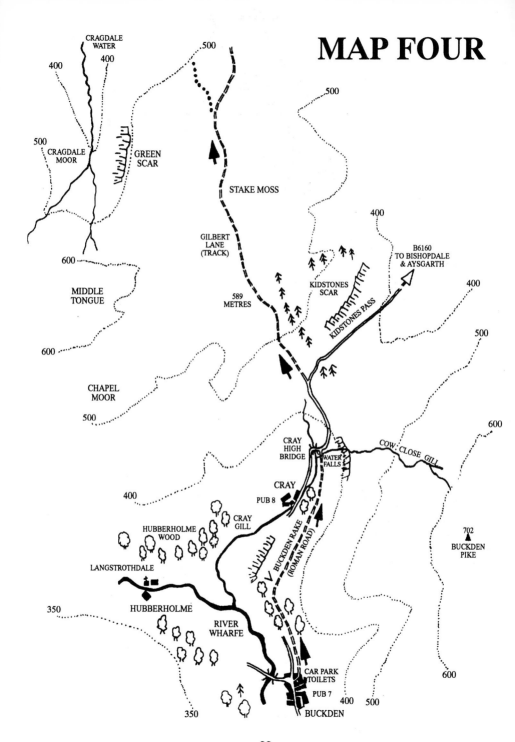

MAP FOUR

CRAGDALE
WATER

400   400

100

500
CRAGDALE
MOOR

GREEN
SCAR

.500

500

STAKE MOSS

GILBERT
LANE
(TRACK)

400

B6160
TO BISHOPDALE
& AYSGARTH

400

600

MIDDLE
TONGUE

589
METRES

KIDSTONES
SCAR

KIDSTONES PASS

500

600

CHAPEL
MOOR

500

600

CRAY
HIGH
BRIDGE

COW CLOSE GILL

WATER
FALLS

CRAY

400

PUB 8

702
BUCKDEN
PIKE

CRAY
GILL

BUCKDEN RAKE
(ROMAN ROAD)

HUBBERHOLME
WOOD

LANGSTROTHDALE

350

HUBBERHOLME

RIVER
WHARFE

350

CAR PARK
TOILETS

PUB 7

400   500

600

BUCKDEN

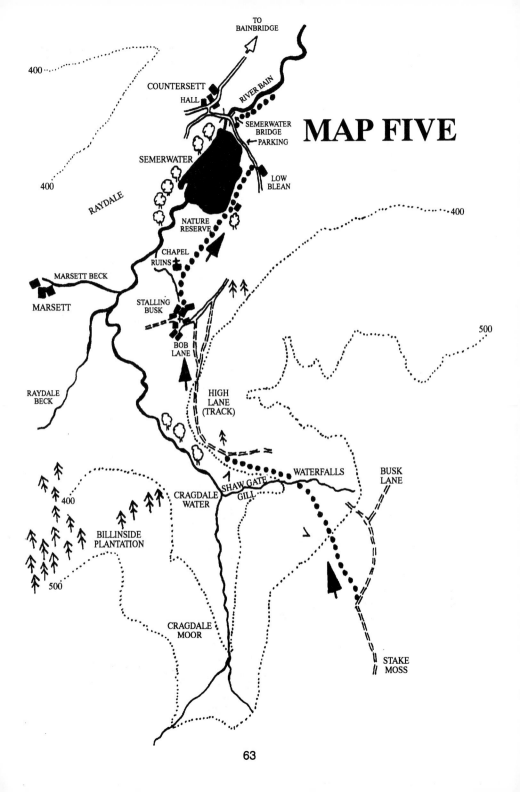

TO
BAINBRIDGE

COUNTERSETT

HALL

RIVER BAIN

SEMERWATER
BRIDGE

PARKING

400

400

RAYDALE

SEMERWATER

LOW
BLEAN

NATURE
RESERVE

400

CHAPEL
RUINS

MARSETT BECK

MARSETT

STALLING
BUSK

BOB
LANE

RAYDALE
BECK

HIGH
LANE
(TRACK)

500

WATERFALLS

BUSK
LANE

400

SHAW GATE

CRAGDALE
WATER

GILL

BILLINSIDE
PLANTATION

500

CRAGDALE
MOOR

STAKE
MOSS

MAP FIVE

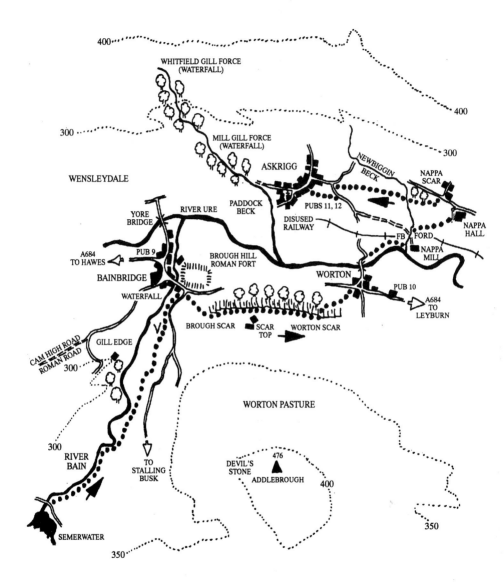

MAP SIX

CRAY is a tiny hamlet with a lovely old inn, a couple of farmhouses and one or two tumbledown barns. Cray's main claim to fame are the spectacular series of waterfalls. *"....Cray, its inn and single farmhouse perched solitary on the brink of a wooded, deep ravine. To sleep in this inn is to awake next morning to a sense of spacious ease. The air blows sweet from the massive bulk of Buckden Pike; and everywhere there is the roar and bubble of descending waters. Cray holds its own among all Wharfe's secluded corners, a hamlet instinct with perculiar charm. From the pasture lands above the inn, where grey, stone fences stride to the further skies, you look down-dale on Buckden."* (H.Sutcliffe 'The Striding Dales' 1929). The track from Cray, over Stake Moss to Bainbridge follows the route of the Roman road from Ilkley. This walk is one of the most spectacular in all of England crossing wild moorland and desolate valleys that are the preserve of the walker. There is a particularly delightful spot to rest beside a small waterfall along Shaw Gate Gill - nothing but the sound of cascading water, bird song and bleating sheep. *"This green track is a walkers' way par excellence. The signpost says: 'Bainbridge'. Wisely, it omits the distance, for once you are on your way, you lose count of the miles; your measure is the succession of glorious panoramas which greet you, one after another, as you go with the wind across the wild uplands."* (A.Wainwright 'A Pennine Journey - The Story of a Long Walk in 1938' 1986).

RAYDALE, meaning 'roebuck valley' was once part of the hunting forest which belonged to the Lords of Middleham Castle. It is closed in by high fells and often experiences sudden changes in weather; the first falls of snow in Wensleydale are often on Drumaldrace and Fleet Moss. *"There is a crystallized beauty about this valley of Raydale, a perfection which is almost exotic."* (E.Pontefract & M.Hartley 'Wensleydale' 1936). This dale was first settled by Scandinavian farmers over 1,000 years ago as the place-names testify - Marsett and Countersett are derived from the Old Norse word 'saetr' meaning 'summer pastures'.

STALLING BUSK, known locally as Busk, enjoys an elevated position at 1100 feet above sea level (336m) and has good views of the dale; the locals say that Stalling Busk is on the money side of the dale whilst Marsett is on the sunny side. *"Frank Outhwaite told me 'They always used to say to the folk at Busk - you've to pay more to be on t'grandstand.' For two months of the year, the sun does not shine directly on Raydale House because 'it's that much under t'hill.' "* (W.R.Mitchell 'High Dale Country' 1991). The ruined church was built in 1603 and had its last burial in the 1980's, although it was replaced by the more modern St Matthews Church in Stalling Busk in 1909. This ruinous building in such peaceful surroundings evokes a sense of eternal peace.

SEMERWATER has the distinction of being one of only three large natural sheets of water in Yorkshire, its lovely setting even inspired Turner to paint it. Semerwater is not as grand as any of the Cumbrian lakes, but history and legend make it a fascinating place. *".... so I made a detour to see it....It is a flooded field."* (A.Wainwright 1986). Semerwater is a glacial lake, a remnant of the last Ice Age when a moraine of debris left by the retreating Wensleydale glacier held back melt waters. A river has now made a channel through this moraine to join Semerwater with the Ure; this is the River Bain, the shortest river in England. The lake is home to many different species of migratory birds and the surrounding marshland supports a great variety of rare plants, consequently the whole area has been designated as a Site of Special Scientific Interest. The Yorkshire Wildlife Trust manages 55 acres of this land as a nature reserve.

There are two legends associated with Semerwater; the first concerns the Carlow Stone (the large boulder of Shap granite brought down by the ice) which can be found on the shore of Semerwater. A giant, who was standing on top of

Addlebrough, dropped the Carlow Stone as he hurled it at the Devil who was stood on Crag Hill. The Devil retaliated, however his stone fell short of the summit of Addlebrough; this stone is known as the Devil's stone. The second legend describes how once a large, prosperous and beautiful city stood where the lake is now. An angel, dressed as a poor man tried in vain to find shelter in the city. Eventually he came across a tumbledown house outside the city in which a poor couple lived where he was fed and given a bed for the night. The next morning he thanked the couple and turned to the city in the distance and cried :-

'Semerwater rise, Semerwater sink,
And cover all save this li'le house
That gave me meat and drink.'

" *Then the earth made a hissing noise, the stream grew into a large lake, and the city was no more. Yet unto this day the natives tell us that the roofs of the buried city are ofttimes seen deep down in the limpid waters.* " (E.Bogg 'From Eden Vale to the Plains of York'). There may be some truth in this because when the level of the lake was lowered in 1937 evidence of pile dwellings and Bronze and Iron Age artefacts were discovered. An old local tradition is for couples to visit the stone soon after they have been engaged; touching the stone supposedly brings good fortune and many healthy children.

BAINBRIDGE is a picturesque village with a spacious green complete with stocks, a pub (Rose & Crown) which reputedly dates back to 1445 and a pleasant series of waterfalls near to the road bridge which provided power for two mills, one of which has been restored and is open to the public. *"We soon come to the broad and cheerful green, surrounded by a picturesque scattering of old but well preserved cottages; for Bainbridge has sufficient charms to make it a pleasant inland resort for holiday times that is quite ideal for those who are content to abandon the sea. The overflow from Semmerwater, which is called the Bain, fills the village with its music as it falls over ledges of rock in* *many cascades along one side of the green."* (G.Home 'Yorkshire' 1908).

There is more to Bainbridge than meets the eye; the small hill to the east of the village, known as Brough Hill, was the site of a Roman fort (Virosidum) which was built by Agricola circa AD80 and occupied for the next 300 years. *"Good was their choice, for with enemies on every side among the wild hills, it would be held impregnable, in spite of many desperate attempts made upon it, in fact, this district has been a stern battling-ground, and one can almost catch the sound of arms clashing and welling up from the aisles of old time."* (E.Bogg 'Beautiful Wensleydale' 1925). It housed up to 500 men and helped control the wild Pennine uplands with its Brigantian population, although the fort was attacked and rebuilt several times. Two Roman roads which lead from the camp have been traced, one goes to Ribchester via Ingleton and cuts an impressive straight course across Wether Fell, the other leads over Stake Pass to Ilkley. *"One of the loveliest views of the village is from Brough Hill...the site of the Roman fort. Looking east from the summit you see the grace of Wensleydale. It is worth while climbing it in the early morning after heavy rain for a sight of the flooded valley. It is a fine view-point, easily reached, which is probably why the Romans chose it."* (E.Pontefract & M.Hartley 1936).

In Medieval times Bainbridge was on the edge of the hunting forest of Wensleydale that stretched from the River Bain to Mallerstang and was home to twelve foresters and their families. Wolves, wild boars and bears roamed the forest, while eagles soared above making it a dangerous place to be after dark, so much so that a law was passed which stated that a horn was to be blown every evening from the Feast of Holy Rood (Sept. 27th) to Shrovetide to guide travellers to the safety of the village. This custom still remains today. *"In the most savage recesses still lurked the bear, and the wild boar found a* safe hiding place. *At that period wolves were numerous, and woe to the benighted traveller if overtaken by a pack of those hungry animals. Herds of deer, and troops of half-wild hogs, and oxen inhabitated the softer and more luxuriant glades by the river's brink.......the forest horn is sounded, as a signal to the benighted travellers who may have lost their way amongst the mountains.*" (E.Bogg). In 1663 villagers bought the manorial rights of Bainbridge from the City of London, this survives today in the form of the locally elected Lords Trustees of the Manor of Bainbridge whose main responsibility is the maintenance of the village green. The 18th century Yore Bridge that spans the River Ure was designed by the famous designer John Carr, who also designed Harewood House near Leeds.

WORTON, pronounced 'Werton', is a small hamlet situated along the main road through the dale. A closer look will reveal some beautiful old houses including Worton Hall dated 1600 said to be the oldest house in Wensleydale. Worton's main claim to fame is the Bread Riot of 1757 when local people, annoyed at the high price of corn, attacked a delivery of corn that was destined for the more affluent gentlemen of the upper dale. The village pub, the Victoria Arms, is well worth the short diversion along the busy road, for this is one of the few remaining unspoilt pubs left in the Dales. As well as serving an excellent pint of ale the landlord also keeps a flock of sheep, a reminder of the days when most landlords of country inns would have had a smallholding to supplement their income.

NAPPA HALL was built circa 1450 by Thomas Metcalfe as a fortified house on 400 acres of land which had been given to his family by Sir Richard Scrope of Bolton Castle in the 15th century for the bravery of James Metcalfe at the battle of Agincourt. James the First and Mary Queen of Scots are reputed to have stayed here. "*A characteristic Wensleydale house is the fifteenth century Nappa Hall, overlooking the Ure near*

Askrigg, and characteristic of the district are its legends. Here Mary, Queen of Scots, spent two days on a visit to Sir Christopher Metcalfe, then head of the famous dale family to which Nappa belonged, and here her ghost is said to have been frequently seen - one of its appearances, in fact, was so real to a lady who was visiting the house at the time that she wrote a detailed account of the occurrence." (Fletcher 'Nooks & Corners of Yorkshire').

The Metcalfes were a very important family in Wensleydale, holding important positions for generations, including High Sheriff of Yorkshire and Master Forester of the forests of Wensleydale; they even had their own chapel within Askrigg church. By the end of the 18th century the Hall had fallen into disrepair and the power of the family had dwindled; today the Hall is still owned by a Metcalfe and is a working farm and bed & breakfast. The Metcalfe name has had a strong presence in Wensleydale since the 12th century and continues to be a common surname today.

ASKRIGG is a fascinating place; to appreciate it fully you must spend time exploring. *"Askrigg seen from a distance is one of the pictures in Wensleydale which never lose their freshness....Seeing it in winter across the snow-covered valley, the walls of the houses show dark against the surrounding whiteness, like children in cosy caps, and only the cottage lights twinkling in the frosty air tell of its reality. From far and near there is an enchantment in the view, so that you enter Askrigg with anticipation. And you are not disappointed."* (E.Pontefract & M.Hartley 1936).

'Ascric', meaning 'ash ridge', was mentioned in the Doomsday book and grew as a trading centre on the edge of the old forest of Wensleydale, as it lay outside the forest boundaries the village was exempt from the strict Norman forest laws. A market charter was granted in 1587, and the Lancaster to Richmond turnpike road came through Askrigg in 1751, however by the turn of the 19th century the market had lapsed and Hawes gradually began to take over as the capital of the upper dale. Askrigg's heyday was in the 18th and early 19th centuries when lead mining, textile production (Askrigg had three mills) and clock making was at its height. Clock making began in Askrigg in the early 17th century, and lasted up until the last shop closed in 1936. Originally the clocks only had hour hands as the Dales people were not interested in minutes. The impressive 18th and 19th century three storey buildings which line the main street testify to this early growth as a town rather than a sleepy, rural village. Close to the market cross, with its bull-ring still set into the cobbles, stood Askrigg Old Hall. This Hall was built in 1678 and had a second floor wooden gallery which was used to watch the bull baiting below. Sadly this house, described as one of the treasures of Wensleydale, was destroyed by fire in 1935. *"....with it's many windows bearing an impress of some antiquated residence of bygone London".* (E.Bogg).

There are two spectacular waterfalls, Mill Gill Force and Whitfield Gill Force, a short distance from the centre of Askrigg, both of which are set in a steep-sided wooded ravine. These waterfalls are caused by the Yoredale Series of rocks, which are comprised of layers of sandstone, limestone, slates and mineral bearing rocks sandwiched together and therefore eroding at varying rates. *"There is a beautiful walk from Askrigg to Mill Gill Force. The distance is scarcely more than half a mile across sloping pastures and through the curious stiles that appear in the stone walls. So dense is the growth of trees in the little ravine that one hears the sound of the waters close at hand without seeing anything but the profusion of foliage overhanging and growing among the rocks. After climbing down among the moist ferns and moss-grown stones, the gushing cascades appear suddenly set in a frame of such lavish beauty that they hold a high place among their rivals in the dale."* (G.Home 1908). To reach the falls follow the lane past the 15th century church, *"....a ramble among the tombs will afford epitaphs of an eccentric character. One, for example, to the memory of Myles Alderson, who died in 1746, states that he was 'an honest attorney'."* (W.Andrews 'Picturesque Yorkshire'). Askrigg Church, dedicated to St Oswald, is the largest church in the dale serving several communities. This site has been a place of worship since at least 1180 as this area was where the Cistercian monks of Jervaulx first attempted to found their monastery before moving further down the dale due to the harsh climate at Askirgg. The church retains many features including an ancient font and a fine ceiling supported by huge beams.

Askrigg has the distinction of being the first village in Yorkshire and one of the first in England to be lit by electricity; power was generated by a turbine attached to one of the mill wheels, *"-Ye Gods ! - by the Lightning's applied force - Electricity"*. (E.Bogg 1925). Askrigg was also the setting for the TV series 'All Creatures Great and Small'; the house opposite the church being 'Skeldale House' and the King's Arms the 'Drovers Inn', where fascinating photographs taken during filming adorn the walls. All of this combines together to make the finest village in the Dales.

ASKRIGG TO REETH

✦

" Every person has a favourite place where they linger; this may be a deserted beach, a mountain peak or the centre of a bustling city. For me this place is Swaledale. No where in the world can rival its rugged beauty. Majestic fells sweep down to meet the bubbling, cascading river, hidden gills beckon you to explore their secrets and time mellowed stone villages compliment the scenery to perfection. To stand on the flanks of Kisdon hill and look out across the roofs of Muker towards Gunnerside fills you with a sense of well being and fulfillment which is beyond words - you have to experience it. And once you have you will be totally captivated by the overwhelming splendour of Swaledale."

Mark Reid 1995.

WALK INFORMATION

Points of interest : A Haunted bridge, the Corpse Way, hay meadows, Viking settlements, hidden treasure, the legacy of the lead mining industry and probably the most beautiful valley in the world.

Distance:

Askrigg to Gunnerside	6 miles
Gunnerside to Reeth	7 miles
Total	13 miles

Time: Allow 7 hours

Terrain: Section from Askrigg to Gunnerside is along exposed moorland roads/farm tracks and across riverside meadowland (firm ground). The climb out of Askrigg is quite steep. The section from Gunnerside to Reeth crosses meadowland and heather moorland. The path is not clearly defined in places and can be very exposed especially on Harkerside Moor (long grass/heather, sometimes boggy).

Ascent: 275 metres. Max. height 500 metres.

Viewpoints: Climb out of Askrigg affords good views over Askrigg and Wensleydale.
Descent through Oxnop Gill looking across Swaledale.
View from road near to Bank Heads Farm and Birks End Farm.
Descent from Harkerside Moor towards Reeth.

FACILITIES

Askrigg	Inn / B&B / Shop / P.O. / Cafe / Bus / Phone / Toilets / Info /
Ivelet	Phone
Gunnerside	Inn / B&B / Shop / P.O. / Cafe / Bus / Phone / Toilets / Info
Reeth	Inn / B&B / Shop / P.O. / Cafe / Bus / Phone / Toilets / Info

ROUTE DESCRIPTION

(Map Seven)

Walk up the main street from the centre of Askrigg and take the road to the left after the 'Crown' pub (road sign 'Muker'). Follow the steep hill all the way to the top along the road (SP to Muker). After crossing the cattle grid at the summit, follow the unfenced road across the moorland for approx. 1 mile until you reach a 'chevron' road sign, take the right fork in the road. This track skirts Oxnop Gill dropping down towards Swaledale. Continue along this track for approx. 2 miles passing through four gates. After Gill Head Farm you pass through a fifth gate near to a ruined barn (NB the gate is missing); where the wall on your left rejoins the track, take the gate leading downhill through this wall. Walk across the field bearing slightly to the right (head towards the telegraph pole in the centre of the field) to reach a wall gate, then straight on to the road. Turn left along the road, then first right down to Ivelet bridge.

(Map Eight)

Cross Ivelet bridge, follow the road to the right up into Ivelet village. Turn right at the telephone box (SP 'Gunnerside'), cross a footbridge and then follow the very clear path all the way to

Gunnerside through a series of wall gaps across meadowland. Leave Gunnerside along the road (road sign 'Muker, Kirkby Stephen'), cross the bridge over the Swale and walk up the road. Take the steps in the wall to your left before you reach the barn, then head left along the track past the green caravans. The path continues through the metal gate in the fence on your right after the caravans (SP 'Bank Heads'). Head across the field to the wall gap in the middle of the field, then follow the well marked path straight ahead, through wall gaps and over stiles, for approx. 3/4 mile until Bank Heads Farm appears up to your right. Follow the grassy track up towards the farm and through a wall gate to the right of the farm that leads onto the road, then walk left along the road for approx. 1/2 mile. Take the second path marked with a FP sign to your left (after Mudd House with its cattle grid). Continue straight on through several wall gates - ignore wall gate to the left in the last field before the road - head straight on to join the road. Turn left along the road, then almost immediately take the FP to your right past the waterfalls. Cross the FB behind the waterfalls and continue through the wall gate on the left. Walk straight ahead across the field (ignore wall gap to the left) to reach another wall gate, continue straight on across the next field over a stile then bear right up the side of the hill over more stiles to reach Hops House Farm. Walk up the steps to the left of the house and cross the ford forsaking the farm track for the stone wall stile directly ahead. Walk across the field to reach Birks End, head left behind the barns and turn right along the track which leads up to the road.

(Map Nine)

Turn left and follow the road for 1/4 mile. When the road bends to the left, take the path to the right through a gate (BW). Follow the clear path through several gates heading straight on across the moor, passing a coniferous plantation on your left. When you reach the second plantation (after 9 gates) bear slightly to your right across the heather moorland (path unclear) until you reach the wall; the wall gate is towards the top of the field, marked by a solitary tree. Continue straight on across a stream along a grassy track over heather moorland, until you join a very clear gravel farm track; follow this track downhill to reach the road. Turn right along the road until you reach Harkerside Place (farm) and follow the FP sign to the left (SP 'Reeth via swing bridge'). Cross the stile into the farmyard, take the gate to the right and head along the track until you reach a gate on your left (clearly marked) near to some ruinous farm buildings. Walk towards Reeth, through wall gaps and follow the clear path towards the suspension bridge. Cross the bridge, turn right and follow the clear path across the field towards the barns. Follow the track up to join the road which leads straight into Reeth.

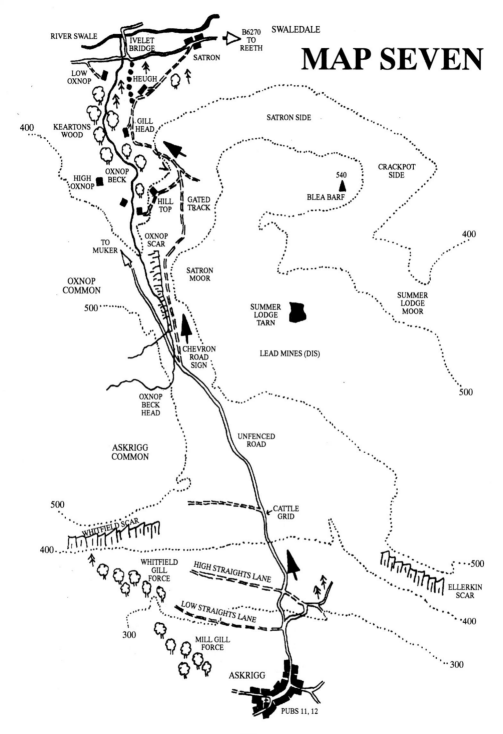

MAP EIGHT

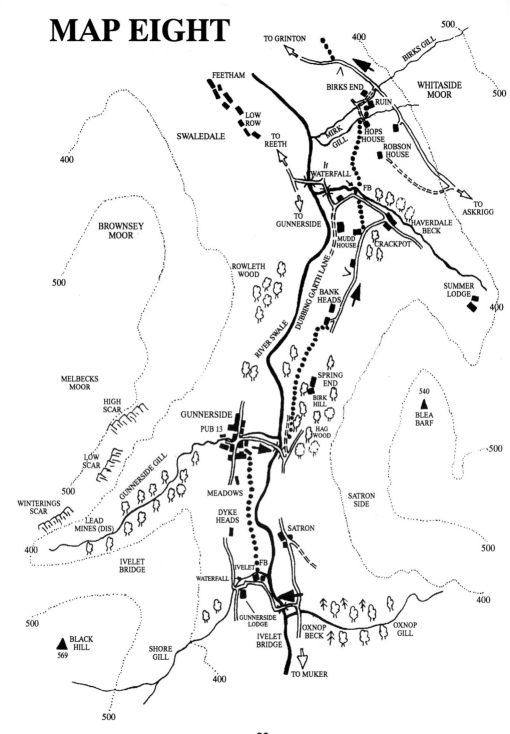

TO GRINTON

400

500

BIRKS GILL

FEETHAM

WHITASIDE MOOR

500

BIRKS END

RUIN

LOW ROW

MIRK GILL

HOPS HOUSE

SWALEDALE

TO REETH

ROBSON HOUSE

WATERFALL

TO ASKRIGG

400

FB

TO GUNNERSIDE

HAVERDALE BECK

BROWNSEY MOOR

MUDD HOUSE

CRACKPOT

500

ROWLETH WOOD

SUMMER LODGE

400

BANK HEADS

DUBBING GARTH LANE

RIVER SWALE

MELBECKS MOOR

SPRING END

540

BLEA BARF

HIGH SCAR

BIRK HILL

GUNNERSIDE

500

PUB 13

HAG WOOD

LOW SCAR

GUNNERSIDE GILL

MEADOWS

SATRON SIDE

WINTERINGS SCAR

LEAD MINES (DIS)

DYKE HEADS

SATRON

500

400

IVELET BRIDGE

IVELET

FB

WATERFALL

BLACK HILL

569

SHORE GILL

GUNNERSIDE LODGE

IVELET BRIDGE

OXNOP BECK

OXNOP GILL

400

500

TO MUKER

400

500

80

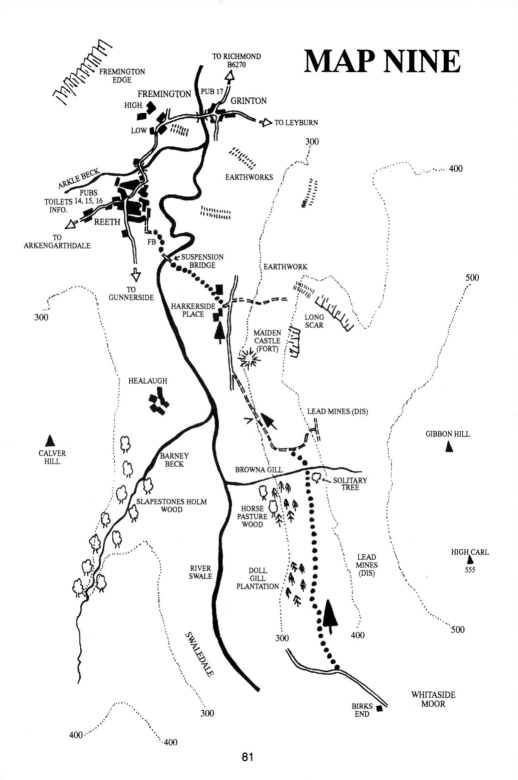

FREMINGTON EDGE

FREMINGTON

HIGH

LOW

PUB 17

TO RICHMOND B6270

GRINTON

TO LEYBURN

EARTHWORKS

300

400

ARKLE BECK

PUBS

TOILETS 14, 15, 16
INFO.

REETH

TO
ARKENGARTHDALE

FB

SUSPENSION
BRIDGE

EARTHWORK

TO
GUNNERSIDE

HARKERSIDE
PLACE

LONG
SCAR

500

300

MAIDEN
CASTLE
(FORT)

HEALAUGH

LEAD MINES (DIS)

GIBBON HILL

CALVER
HILL

BARNEY
BECK

BROWNA GILL

SOLITARY
TREE

SLAPESTONES HOLM
WOOD

HORSE
PASTURE
WOOD

LEAD
MINES
(DIS)

HIGH CARL

555

RIVER
SWALE

DOLL
GILL
PLANTATION

300

400

500

SWALEDALE

300

WHITASIDE
MOOR

400

400

BIRKS
END

81

"Neither Arkengarthdale nor Swaledale have yet been fully discovered by tourists. That is their loss, for Swaledale is one of the proudest possessions of the county. The good road that winds the length of the dale, now climbing, now dropping, ever crossing and recrossing the turbulent Swale, provides country that is a veritable feast for the eye." (J.&.R Fairfax-Blakeborough 'The Spirit of Yorkshire' 1954.)

OXNOP GILL is a little known tributary of Swaledale (pronounced 'Swardill' locally) but boasts magnificent limestone scenery, *"....my own road was taking me rapidly down into the valley, through a rocky boulder-strewn gorge with a most impressive wall of crags above on the right."* (A.Wainwright 'A Pennine Journey - The Story of a Long Walk in 1938' 1986). This road was once a busy route between the two dales, indeed near to the cattle grid on the road once stood 'Jenkin Gate' which was a popular inn with both the local mining community and travellers. The whole walk from Askrigg to Ivelet is an absolute delight with far-reaching views across Wensleydale from Askrigg Common that takes in, on a clear day, Great Whernside, Buckden Pike, Addlebrough, Raydale, Semerwater and much of Wensleydale - breathe in deeply and capture this swathe of England in your mind's eye forever. Expansive moorland soon gives way to the rich greens of Swaledale, with views of this wonderful valley opening up with every step. *"Swaledale was in front now, unfolding a little more of its beauty with every step I took......I could see copse and woodland, rich meadow and pleasant pasture wonderfully blended in the shades of soaring hill and ragged peak, and my heart warmed at the sight."* (A.Wainwright 1986). There are some good examples of long-house farms in Oxnop, which were designed so that house and barn are all under the same roof. This building style dates back to the Vikings; many Norse traditions, place names and farming techniques survive in one form or another in the upper reaches of the dales, *"It is said that up until the sixteenth century a Norse speech lingered in the remoter corners of Upper*

Swaledale and Wensleydale, strongly enough for a dalesman to have made himself understood to a Norwegian." (E.Pontefract & M.Hartley 'Yorkshire Tour' 1939). The dialect in the area today is still strong and contains many words associated with old Norse.

IVELET BRIDGE crosses the fastest flowing river in England - the Swale. This is one of the best examples of a packhorse bridge in the Dales with a single, graceful high arch, *"...like a rainbow set in stone."* (W.Mitchell 'High Dale Country' 1991); it is also steeped in history and legend. The 'Corpse Way' passes the bridge en route from Keld to Grinton. Before a church was built at Muker in 1580 the people of the upper dale had to carry their dead to the burial ground at Grinton, a 12 mile journey which could take two days. This journey originally stemmed from Norse mythology in which the 'corpse way' mirrored the last journey of the soul from earth to the next life. The dead were carried in wicker baskets and wrapped in a shroud, stone slabs were placed along the route on which the coffin could be rested, an example of which survives today at the north end of Ivelet Bridge. *"At Riddings Farm, near Feetham, a barn still known as Dead House is pointed out as the place where mourners would often leave their burden overnight; this gave them a chance to spend a convivial evening at the neighbouring Punch Bowl Inn."* (G.B.Wood 'Yorkshire Tribute' 1950) - well, why not? The bridge is reputedly haunted by a headless black dog, which will bring misfortune if you see it. *"The dog was always seen gliding on to the bridge, where it would disappear over the edge."* (E.Pontefract & M.Hartley 'Swaledale' 1934). The tiny hamlet of Ivelet is dominated by the imposing Gunnerside Lodge, a shooting lodge once owned by Lord Peel.

The hay meadows between Ivelet and Gunnerside are abundant with wild flowers and grasses (over 20 different species); these fields truly are traditional meadows. To walk through these in June is an experience not to be missed. *"It makes an unforgettable Alpine-like picture, and once you have seen it no amount of grey weather can efface it from your mind."* (E.Pontefract & M.Hartley 1939).

GUNNERSIDE originated as a small Norse farming settlement (Gunnar's pastures), as the steep fells and narrow valley floor would have reminded those early settlers of home. They brought with them a tradition of sheep farming on the fells, with cattle farming and haymaking on the lower pastures. This survives today in the form of numerous field barns along the valley floor with miles of stone walls dividing small fields, and vast areas of open moorland. Gunnerside remained virtually unchanged until the development of the lead mining industry on the moors and in the gills behind the village in the 18th century. Lead mining first began in Swaledale during Roman times, but reached its height between 1790 and 1860 when Swaledale produced around 6000 tonnes annually. Lead from these mines was used as early as the 12th century to roof French abbeys and the King's castle at Windsor; many cathedrals in Rome and castles in Germany have Swaledale lead on their roofs. Gunnerside Gill and the Old Gang Mines are fascinating places to explore and gain an insight into this early contribution to the industrial revolution. *"The men worked under conditions which would not be allowed to-day. They descended the shafts in complete darkness by ladders on either side, the last man pulling the door to after him....One man was not careful to knock all the snow from his clogs, and as he shut the door behind him he slipped and hurtled to the bottom."* (E.Pontefract & M.Hartley 1934). By the end of the 19th century competition from abroad caused the demise of this industry and the miners cottages fell into disrepair, however the increasing popularity of Swaledale as a tourist centre has given a new lease of life to them as holiday homes. There is, however, one unique reminder of this almost forgotten industry. Calvert's Blacksmith's Shop is still in business, as it has been since at least 1840, and remains completely unaltered with old lead mining implements hanging around the furnace and even a casting mould for the pigs of lead still with its inscription of 'Old Gang'.

I recommend that you take time to explore as there is more to Gunnerside than meets the eye. It is not a particularly pretty village, the houses are basic and functional, yet there is a melancholy feeling about the place - it exudes the 'spirit' of Swaledale. Tiny stone cottages cluster around small 'greens', huddled together as if for protection against the elements and the harsh surroundings. Look into the heart of the village and you will see an active community with school, shop, Post Office, chapel, pub, cafe and even a small brewery! *"But all beyond Reeth is a wilderness of hill, moor, torrent, crag, and heather-clad expanse. In summer the becks and waterfalls, each with its setting of grey rock and green fern, are haunts of beauty and of music; in winter, when the waters come pouring down from the hills in mighty torrents they are apt to strike awe into the hearts of folk who have never seen anything but a placid river."* (Fletcher 'Nooks & Corners of Yorkshire').

CRACKPOT is a small farming hamlet whose curious name comes from old Norse meaning 'ravine where crows abound'. Swaledale is famous for its waterfalls, *"In Swaledale it is always the sound of falling water which call back one's wandering thoughts. I have paused to rest beside a little stream of wondrous beauty. Across the field, where two or three ashes grew together in a clump, I first saw it gleaming silver in the shadow; and a little lower down it ran beneath a bridge in the prettiest cascade imaginable. The fall was of trifling height, no more than three or four feet; but the water shot over it in a curve so full and copious and fell into so brown a pool below, beneath banks so cool and mossy, that there was more delight in watching it than one finds in many a stream of far greater volume."* (A.Norway 'Highways and Byways in Yorkshire' 1899). There are a very picturesque series of waterfalls along the Haverdale Beck near to Crackpot.

MAIDEN CASTLE was built circa 70 AD by the Celtic Brigantes as a defensive site to prevent the Roman Legions from spreading into the dale. This proved unsuccessful as it was later used by the Romans as a halting place and look-out due to its position near to the route of the Roman road from Bainbridge to Greta Bridge. It consists of a rectangular depression in the hillside some 70 metres across, with earth ramparts and a deep ditch. The site is approached by an avenue of stones laid in parallel lines that were once possibly used as defensive walls. There are also two Tumulus in the area, under one of which is reputedly buried a fortune in gold. *"Tradition has it that a chest of gold lies buried under the first mound, and many have searched for it. We found an old spade on one side with its edges curled over, which might have been left by some disconsolate digger."* (E.Pontefract & M.Hartley 1934). Maiden Castle can be found 100 yards up to the right on the heather moorland where the gravel track and the road meet after the descent from Harkerside moor.

REETH occupies a commanding position on the flanks of Calver hill at the point where Arkengarthdale and Swaledale meet. *"...Reeth, a small and picturesque town lying at the foot of Calver Hill and surrounded on all sides by wild and wide-spreading moors, claims to be the capital of Swaledale.....It is at this point that Swaledale becomes as savage in its scenery as the most desolate of Highland glens. Standing on Calver Hill one may look across a truly impressive stretch of dale and moor. The valley of the Swale lies in front..."* (Fletcher). This prominant position led to Reeth being granted a market charter in 1695, the village continued to grow during the 18th and 19th centuries as a centre for the lead mining and hand knitting industries which thrived in the dale during this period; the many fine Georgian buildings which line the spacious green testify to this growth. In its heyday Reeth supported seven fairs, a weekly market and a population three times greater than that of today; there were even plans to extend the branch line from Richmond to bring the railway to Reeth. However by the end of the 19th century the mines had closed and many people left for work in the mills of Lancashire or the pits of Newcastle. Grass has grown over much of the old cobbled market place, although the weekly Friday market has recently been revived and the September Reeth Show still flourishes. *"It must have thrived with the lead-mines in Arkengarthdale and along the Swale, for it has gone back since the period of its former prosperity, and is glad of the fact that its situation, and the cheerful green which the houses look upon, have made it something of a holiday resort."* (G.Home 'Yorkshire' 1908).

In 1785 'Reeth Friends' School' was founded by the Quakers, which provided free education in the three 'R's' and also taught mining, surveying and geology; the school survived until 1939. An endowment established by the Quakers provides funds for the County Council School, which is still known as the 'Reeth Friends' School'. The present school was built in 1862 as a replacement for the old Quaker school, its prominant site chosen so that it could be seen from all of the parishes it served. Reeth has matured and mellowed over the years into what could be described as the perfect English country village; a large sloping village green surrounded by ancient inns, greystone houses and shops with enticing alleys leading off the green beckoning you to explore, all in a unsurpassable setting of river and moorland; Reeth is the jewel in the crown of Swaledale. *"Clustering round the spacious green on a sunny slope are the grey old houses and inns of this little Swaledale town,....From the peace memorial on the green we see all the grandeur of its setting, with wooded hills and bare moorland heights on every hand, their heads often lost in clouds."* (A.Mee 'Yorkshire North Riding' 1941).

The Swaledale Folk Museum, which is housed in the old Methodist Sunday School, is well worth a visit to see the many lead mining and farming implements of by-gone days and to gain an insight into local history. Reeth was James Herriot's 'Darrowby' in the film version of 'It shouldn't happen to a Vet'; The imposing house at the top left hand corner of the green was 'Skeldale House' and the Black Bull doubled as the 'Drover's Arms'; the frontage of the Black Bull was originally part of a Georgian drapers shop - note the unusual pub sign, the result of a long running planning dispute with the National Park.

ARKENGARTHDALE and the Arkle Beck make up some of the most desolate, wild and magnificent scenery in the Dales. The unusual name originates from 'Arkil's garth', 'Arkil' being the Norse chieftain in the area and 'garth' being his clearing. The road, which winds up the dale, passes many small hamlets with weird and wonderful names most of which are derived from Norse, (Booze, Langthwaite, Eskeleth, Whaw, Faggergill, Punchard) and eventually reaches the lonely Tan Hill Inn (England's highest Inn at 1732 feet) after crossing miles of wild moorland. The fells are scarred with more remains of the lead mining industry than any other dale; this adds to the sombre beauty of the area. *"The high road running through the dale by way of William Gill and Polly Moss leads to as lonely and desolate a tract of country as any one fond of solitude could desire - as lonely as (if not lonelier than) the moors of Bowes and Stainmore, to which it leads."* (Fletcher).

REETH TO WEST BURTON

✦

"I think the exact moment when it dawned on me that Yorkshire was a magical place was when I pulled my car off the unfenced road which leads from Leyburn over Bellerby Moor to Grinton. It was around the highest point, by a little stream, and I looked back over the swelling moorland to the great wooded valley of the Swale where it curves on its approach to Richmond. I gazed at the scene in disbelief. There was everything here; wildness and solitude breathing from the bare fells, yet a hint of softness where the river wound along the valley floor. And in all the green miles around me there was not another human being to be seen. I got out of my car and sat on the springy grass as I have done on countless occasions since then. I was captivated, completely spellbound and I still am to this day."

J.Herriot 'My Yorkshire' 1979.

WALK INFORMATION

. . . .

Points of interest: The 'Cathedral of the Dales', the Castle where Mary Queen of Scots' was held prisoner, Herriot's honeymoon hotel, Garibaldi's red shirts, spectacular waterfalls and the prettiest village in the Dales.

Distance:

Reeth to Carperby	8 miles
Carperby to West Burton	3 miles
Total	11 miles

Time: Allow 5 hours (excluding stops at Castle Bolton & Aysgarth)

Terrain: Between Reeth and Carperby the route follows very clear gravel/turf tracks.
The climb from Grinton to the top of the moor is fairly long and strenuous; Grinton Moor can also be very exposed. The section between Carperby and West Burton is along well marked footpaths which cross meadowland (long grass).

Ascent: 332 metres. Max. height 508 m

Viewpoints: View from Grinton Moor towards Reeth.
Descent towards Castle Bolton.
Aysgarth Falls and waterfalls at West Burton.
View across Bishopdale as you descend towards Eshington Bridge.

FACILITIES

. . . .

Reeth	Inn / B&B / Shop / P.O. / Cafe / Bus / Phone / Toilets / Info
Grinton	Inn / B&B / Phone / Toilets
Castle Bolton	Shop / Cafe / Phone / Toilets
Carperby	Inn / B&B / Bus / Phone
Aysgarth	Inn / B&B / Shop / P.O. / Cafe / Bus / Phone / Toilets / Info
West Burton	Inn / B&B / Shop / P.O. / Bus / Phone

ROUTE DESCRIPTION

. . . .

(Map Ten)

Leave Reeth along the Richmond road, cross the bridge over Arkle Beck and take the FP to the right (SP 'Grinton') just before you enter Fremington. Follow this clear path along the river bank and across the fields to Grinton Bridge. Cross the bridge, pass the church on your right and follow the road straight ahead up the hill (SP 'Leyburn') until you reach a cattle grid. Immediately before the cattle grid take the gate to the right marked FP, follow the unclear path straight up the hill and keep heading upwards through the heather and bracken (no clear path) until a sharp bend in the road (marked by a triangular road sign) becomes visible, head towards this. Follow the unfenced road uphill for approx. 1 mile; ignore tracks to your right marked 'Bridleway only -no vehicles'. When the road levels out follow the track which heads diagonally up to the right (signed BW) across the moorland until you reach the two small stone cairns on the summit of the hill. After the cairns continue across the top of the moor to the left of the fence, through a gate and head along the very clear track down hill for approx. 1 mile until you reach Dent's Houses. Pass the houses on your left and continue up hill until you reach a stile/gate. Cross the stile and follow the green lane.

Continue along the lane, passing a wood on your right until you reach a wall. Go through the gate and follow the walled lane all the way into Castle Bolton. Take the road to the right of the castle, passing the church on your right. Go through the gate and bear left across the field (SP 'Aysgarth') to a wall gate at the bottom end of the wood. The path is clear across fields and over a footbridge all the way to West Bolton Farm. Walk through the farmyard (keep left of the buildings) and take the path on your right (SP) immediately after the farm buildings. Follow this clear path (yellow markers) to the right of the wood and through meadowland to reach East End Farm; (the path joins the road to the left of the stone barn).Turn right along the road into Carperby.

Go through the gate directly opposite the Wheatsheaf pub (SP 'Aysgarth'), after approx 100 yds turn right through the wall gap then follow the path down hill keeping the wall to your left until you reach a lane. The very clear path (SP 'Aysgarth') continues on the opposite side of the lane and crosses meadowland to reach Freeholder's Wood. Bear right through the wood to reach the road. Turn left and follow the road down to the bridge at Aysgarth Falls. Cross the bridge and walk up the steps between the mill and the cottages to St. Andrew's Church. Pass the church on your left and continue straight ahead through the churchyard; this path will bring you out on the main road. The path continues on the opposite side of the road through a wall stile (SP 'Eshington Bridge') and is clearly marked all the way to the bridge. Take the FP (SP 'West Burton') to the right after the bridge and follow this clear path across fields with the river on your right to reach a bend in the river, then head up past the barn and over a stile to the right of a gate that leads on to the road. Take the path on the opposite side of the road which leads into West Burton.

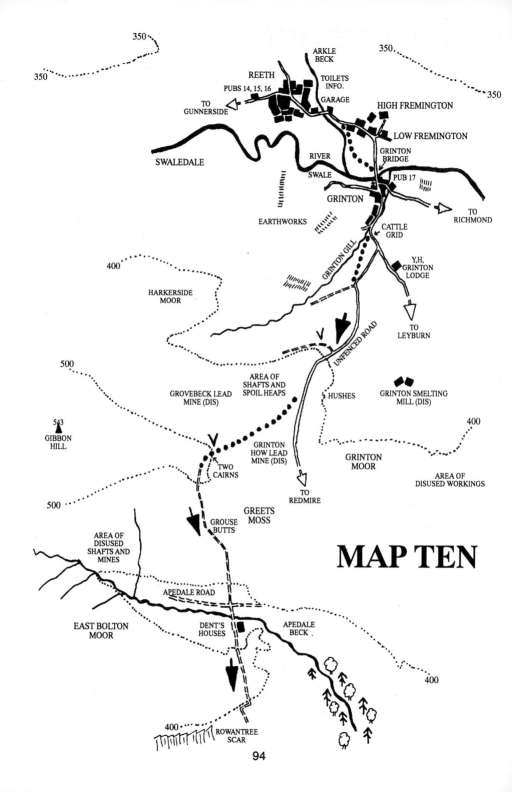

ARKLE
BECK

REETH

TOILETS
INFO.

PUBS 14, 15, 16

GARAGE

HIGH FREMINGTON

TO
GUNNERSIDE

LOW FREMINGTON

GRINTON
BRIDGE

SWALEDALE

RIVER

PUB 17

SWALE

GRINTON

TO
RICHMOND

EARTHWORKS

CATTLE
GRID

350
350
350
350
350

Y.H.
GRINTON
LODGE

400

HARKERSIDE
MOOR

GRINTON GILL

UNFENCED ROAD

TO
LEYBURN

500

AREA OF
SHAFTS AND
SPOIL HEAPS

HUSHES

GRINTON SMELTING
MILL (DIS)

400

GROVEBECK LEAD
MINE (DIS)

543
GIBBON
HILL

GRINTON
HOW LEAD
MINE (DIS)

GRINTON
MOOR

AREA OF
DISUSED WORKINGS

TWO
CAIRNS

500

TO
REDMIRE

GREETS
MOSS

GROUSE
BUTTS

MAP TEN

AREA OF
DISUSED
SHAFTS AND
MINES

APEDALE ROAD

EAST BOLTON
MOOR

DENT'S
HOUSES

APEDALE
BECK

400

400

ROWANTREE
SCAR

94

MAP ELEVEN

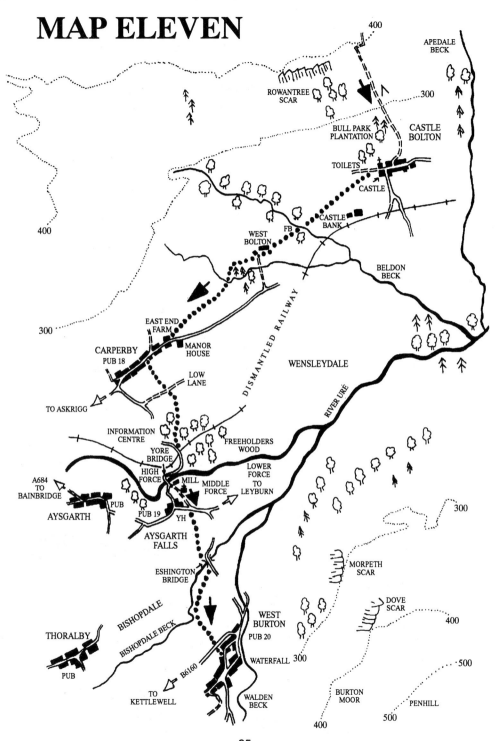

400

APEDALE
BECK

ROWANTREE
SCAR

300

BULL PARK
PLANTATION

CASTLE
BOLTON

TOILETS

CASTLE

400

CASTLE
BANK

WEST
BOLTON

FB

BELDON
BECK

300

DISMANTLED RAILWAY

EAST END
FARM

CARPERBY
PUB 18

MANOR
HOUSE

WENSLEYDALE

LOW
LANE

TO ASKRIGG

RIVER URE

INFORMATION
CENTRE

FREEHOLDERS
WOOD

YORE
BRIDGE

A684
TO
BAINBRIDGE

HIGH
FORCE

MILL

LOWER
FORCE
TO
LEYBURN

MIDDLE
FORCE

300

PUB

PUB 19

YH

AYSGARTH

AYSGARTH
FALLS

ESHINGTON
BRIDGE

MORPETH
SCAR

DOVE
SCAR

BISHOPDALE

400

THORALBY

WEST
BURTON

PUB 20

BISHOPDALE BECK

500

PUB

B6160

WATERFALL

300

TO
KETTLEWELL

WALDEN
BECK

BURTON
MOOR

PENHILL

400

500

GRINTON is a jumble of pretty stone cottages, a sturdy bridge over the Swale, a lovely old pub and the Cathedral of the Dales' - St Andrew's Church. This site has been a place of worship since pre-conquest days, originally for pagan ceremonies later being adopted by the Christian Church, however the first church was built during Norman times. Fragments of the Norman church survive today in the form of part of the chancel arch, a small window and the bowl of the font. The present church dates from the 14th-16th centuries and was built by the monks of Bridlington, although restoration took place in 1896. Up until Tudor times Grinton Church served the whole of Swaledale stretching up to the old Westmorland border, which made it one of the largest parishes in the country. This was the only consecrated ground in Swaledale which meant that the dead had to be carried in wicker baskets for the 12 mile journey from the dale head to the church along the 'Corpse Way'; thankfully a church was built in Muker at 1580. In the 17th century a law was passed to help the declining woollen trade whereby the dead were to be buried in a woollen shroud. Adam Barker, a local man, made the mistake of burying his daughter in a linen shroud in the churchyard at Grinton in 1692 and was subsequently fined £5. As a focal point for such a large catchment area Grinton became an important meeting place, weekly Sunday markets were held here for the benefit of the worshippers despite the fact that the medieval church poured scorn on such non-religious events, especially on a Sunday. Today the church is a place of eternal peace, "*A heavy border of yews running round the churchyard.....seem to gather round as if to protect the church from the storms which sweep down the dale. There is a feeling of age and history in the burial ground; it has gathered to itself from the bounds of a great parish so many sons and daughters of the dale. The grey church tower seems to call its children, the wide aisles on either side to stretch out sheltering arms, and the battlemented clerestory behind to offer security. The church gazes up the dale as it did long centuries ago, watching for those slow processions down the old corpse way.*" (E.Pontefract & M.Hartley 'Swaledale' 1934). It is worth exploring the church as it boasts many interesting features, such as the 'Lepers Squint' which allowed lepers to watch the service from outside, a chained copy of Birkett's New Testament on a 14th century stand, ancient stained glass and grooves in the stonework by the porch where arrows were sharpened by men waiting for their lords who were attending a pre-hunt service!

Perched on Grinton Moor near to the Leyburn road is Grinton Lodge. This 19th century battlemented building was once the shooting lodge of Col. Charlesworth, however it has been a Youth Hostel since the 1940's. Grinton Moor, like so many other moors in Swaledale, is littered with the remains of the lead mining industry; near to Codgen Gill are the remains of an early 19th century smelting mill. This area also affords some of the best views in Swaledale including a bird's eye view of Reeth. "*....the green valley of Arkengarthdale stretches out like a promised land; and there is a glimpse of Swaledale, winding round to the left, just enough to set you longing for its upland regions.*" (E.Pontefract & M.Hartley 1934).

APEDALE (meaning the valley of the Norseman 'Appi') was once a major centre for lead mining in Wensleydale, which has left a legacy of spoil heaps, mine shafts and miles of glorious green lanes and gravel tracks. It is a lonely, desolate and relatively unknown valley whose only occupants are sheep, rabbits and grouse (unfortunately no monkeys!), however if you enjoy wild places then you will fall in love with the haunting beauty of Apedale. "*A moor often has the desolation of death about it, but it teems with life. Put your back against it, and look at the sky, and listen. Listen carefully. Out of the profound stillness comes a magnitude of tiny sounds. There are marching armies in the grass, winged battalions hovering above it. I have seen some fine dramas played amongst the tangled roots of heather. Sudden slaughter, terror, love, hate and passion: all the elements of* *first class drama are presented here. The actors are lilliputian; the stage may be a blade of grass, or the petal of a mountain pansy. But the events you witness are grim; the players are in earnest. Feeling runs pretty high even among crawling pinheads. Next time you have an idle day, make yourself a couch on a quiet moor, and lie down. Sleep, if you are tired. But first, for a while, listen. And learn."* (A.Wainwright 'A Pennine Journey - The Story of a Long Walk in 1938' 1986). It is also interesting to note that the moorland which rises to over 540 metres at the head of Apedale is known as Gibbon Hill - perhaps there are some of our hairy relatives here after all! The descent from Apedale towards Castle Bolton affords superb views across Wensleydale above the ramparts of the castle towards Penhill, Walden, Bishopdale and Addlebrough - a strategic spot indeed.

CASTLE BOLTON, with its old stone cottages lining the green, is compeletly dwarfed by the majestic Bolton Castle. The castle was built in 1379 by Richard le Scrope, the Chancellor of England to Richard II, and took 18 years to complete at a cost of £12,000, an incredible sum of money in those days. Its walls are nine feet thick and stand 130 feet wide by 180 feet long, with four massive corner towers nearly 100 feet high enclosing a central courtyard. It was designed more as a fortified house with comfort in mind than a defensive castle. *"Lord Scrope, High Chancellor of England, obtained King Richard's licence to fortify his manorial residence at Bolton, in the third year of his reign; and eighteen changeful years swept past before the lordly pile was completed at a cost of 18,000 marks. Patient oxen drew the necessary wood from Engleby Forest, in Cumberland, and the masonary of the castle was calculated to withstand leaguer and storm, should evil days of internecine strife trouble the nation."* (W.Andrews 'Bygone Yorkshire' 1892). Many of the galleries and great halls are still supported by these 600 year old oak beams. The stone for the castle came from quarries in Apedale and local legend also tells us that these early builders used Ox blood mixed with the mortar to give it added strength. *"...it had chimneys - at that time revolutionary features in England."* (M.Hartley & J.Ingilby 'The Wonders of Yorkshire' 1959). The castle occupies a commanding position and dominates much of Wensleydale; it can be seen for miles around, *"....but to me the appeal of the castle is in its situation - all-seeing and visible from such great distances, dwarfing its surroundings."* (J.Herriot 'James Herriot's Yorkshire' 1979).

The castle has had a turbulent history and played an important role in the history of England. *"The wind sighed through the ruins with a wailing, melancholy sound; dark patches of storm clouds were swiftly sailing across the heavens, hiding the full-orbed queen of the night, and casting dense shadows on the old fortress, which presented a stern, gloomy, and desolate look almost awe-inspiring. Now and again for a brief few moments the moon rode from behind the jagged clouds, shedding forth, on the stern and silent castle, rays of subdued splendour. As we stood gazing on the mighty structure, with not a sound to disturb our reverie, save that caused by the flight of a solitary night bird, and the wind rustling amongst the ivy and shivering of withered leaves, bygone scenes and actors in life's great drama flit in imagination before our gaze."* (E.Bogg 'From Eden Vale to the Plains of York'). Mary, Queen of Scots was imprisoned in the castle from July 1568 until January 1569 before being taken to Tutbury Castle in Staffordshire. She was treated well during her stay at Bolton Castle, having her own chambers and forty servants, although legend has it that she attempted to escape but was recaptured on Leyburn Shawl at a spot that is now known as 'The Queen's Gap'. The castle played an important role in the English Civil war as a base for the Royalist forces, however Parliamentary forces besieged the castle in 1645 and the Royalists surrendered. The castle was made untenable in 1647, under orders from Cromwell, after which it remained uninhabited for almost three centuries; the weakening of the structure in 1647 contributed to the collapse of the north east tower during a storm in 1761. *"In the battle of Flodden, which ended in a victory for England, the lusty lads of Wensleydale were in the thick of the fight."* (W.Andrews 'Picturesque Yorkshire'). The 13th Lord Scrope died in 1630 from the plague a year or so after surrendering to the Parliamentary forces, after which the estate passed to his son-in-law Charles Powlett, who later became the Duke of Bolton. Further down the dale, near to Wensley, stands Bolton Hall which was built in 1678 by the fourth Duke of Bolton as the family home instead of the ruinous castle; the castle and hall are still owned and occupied by Lord Bolton. I recommend a tour of the castle to see the great halls, chapel, armoury, kitchens and dungeons carved out of solid rock where an arm bone was found still manacled to the dungeon wall.

To the north of the castle stands St Oswald's Church which was built in 1325, pre-dating the castle by almost 70 years. Note the grooves in the stonework beside the door caused by the sharpening of arrows and swords, a reminder of less peaceful times. *"In another position the little church of St Oswald would be a normal size for the village, but, standing close under the castle walls, it seems a toy building, and for most of the day the sun is hidden from it....Probably one of the last instances of public apology took place here. A woman had slandered another, and the apology was demanded by the whole village. During the service she had to walk up and down the aisle, and at the end of it make her apology, which she did in rhyme."* (E.Pontefract & M.Hartley 'Wensleydale' 1936). Close by is the old village post office which makes a perfect 'chocolate box' picture.

CARPERBY is an ancient village which was mentioned in the Domesday Book (then called 'Kerparbi') and has had long traditions of farming and trading. The village was granted a market charter in 1305; there is a fine stepped market cross in the centre of the village dated 1674 complete with some very unusual carvings. Superbly preserved medieval cultivation terraces, or lynchets, can be found in the fields behind the village from days when crops were grown in the dale (hence the name of the pub). The Wensleydale breed of sheep were reputedly first recognised and named here. The impressive Friends' Meeting House dated 1864 indicates the importance of Quakerism in this area. The 'Wheatsheaf Hotel' was the honeymoon hotel of the real life James Herriot in the 1941. *"Our bedroom, with its brass bedstead, looked out over the old roofs of the village across the Ure to the hills beyond, and I still feel that wherever Helen and I might have spent our honeymoon we could not have found greater beauty."* (J.Herriot 1979). Today Carperby is a quiet place with quaint stone cottages lining the road which runs through the village.

FREEHOLDERS' WOOD is a remnant of the ancient woodland that once covered much of Wensleydale. A wide variety of deciduous species can be found here including elm, oak, ash, rowan, birch, wild cherry, holly and hazel covering an area of 32 acres beside Aysgarth Falls. For centuries this wood has been managed on a rotational coppicing basis where trees are cut back to ground level, new shoots are allowed to grow to a usable thickness and then they are harvested; the villagers of Carperby still have rights to gather wood. It is now owned and managed by the Yorkshire Dales National Park who bought it from the Bolton Estate over ten years ago. The wood had been neglected and allowed to grow wild, but they have re-introduced coppicing which has benefited the fauna and flora of the wood (wildlife includes roe deer). The successful management of Freeholders' Wood has led to the Forestry Commission declaring it a woodland centre of excellence. Paths through the wood lead to the Middle and Lower Falls. *"The trees make an archway over the path which leads to the Lower Falls, whose roaring when the river is in flood is heard like thunder long before they are reached. The volume of water tossing and swirling is impressive, though there is terror in its fascination, but these falls are beautiful at all times. With the sound of them in your ears you return along the path. Dusk falls, and the gloom of the wood is intensified. For you the road lies just beyond, but you realize here the difficulties of those early travellers in the forest, and their terror when night was coming on, of being lost."* (E.Pontefract & M.Hartley 1936).

THE WENSLEYDALE RAILWAY once connected the Settle to Carlisle line at Garsdale with the main North East line at Northallerton, but passenger services ceased in 1954 and freight in 1964. At its height in the early 1900's special excursion trains ran from the northern industrial towns and brought people to places such as Hawes, Hardraw and Aysgarth. Cars have now taken the place of the train, as the large car parks above the falls testify. The old railway station and bridge at Aysgarth can still be seen. The section from Northallerton to Redmire is still used by the MOD to transport heavy machinery up tp the ranges on the surrounding moors, but the tracks on the section between Redmire and Garsdale have been torn up. There are efforts to re-open this section - new track has recently been laid to Castle Bolton and passenger services look set to resume.

AYSGARTH FALLS make up one of the tourist 'honeypots' of the Dales, and it easy to understand why. *"Ah, exqusite Aysgarth! Who would not strive and strive again to reach some true expression of the fair picture which lies glowing in his memory! Words are but a palisade, through whose chinks one can, at most, catch some gleam of all that beauty, and while I sit and vainly steep my senses in the roar and turmoil of the flashing water, I know well that I might as easily describe a swallow's flight as the abounding loveliness of this great fall at Aysgarth."* (A.Norway 'Highways and Byways in Yorkshire' 1899). The River Ure tumbles over rock terraces in a series of waterfalls which stretch for over a mile through a beautiful narrow wooded valley, dropping over 200 feet along the way. There are three groupings of falls; the Upper Falls, which have the most attractive setting, are best viewed from the road bridge, but the Middle and Lower Falls are the most spectacular, especially after heavy rain, and can be reached by following the clearly marked paths through Freeholders' Wood. *"It is stirring to come here after a storm and see the River Ure roaring along its stony bed under the trees. Rushing impetuously in a flood hemmed in by limestone walls and overhanging woods, tumbling down rocky ledges like the steps of a giant's staircase, the water breaks into amber foam; and the roar of the river can be heard like the thunder of a thousand horses on Leyburn Shawl six miles away. It was a spectacle that enchanted Turner, and is one of the finest sights in the Dales, which must be seen for its entralling beauty to be believed."* (A.Mee 'Yorkshire North Riding' 1941). Next to the bridge, which originally dates from the late 16th century and widened in 1788, stands Yore Mill. This mill was built in 1784, although destroyed by fire and rebuilt in the 1850's, and has been used as a flour and cotton mill over the years; the red shirts of Garibaldi's army came from here! It now houses the Coach and Carriage Museum.

St Andrew's Church dates mainly from 1866 when rebuilding work took place; some remnants of the original late

12th century church remain in the lower part of the tower. St Andrew's was, for many centuries, the main church in upper Wensleydale and has the largest churchyard in the country. The Aysgarth parish once stretched for 81,000 acres although this has now been sub-divided. *"There is about Aysgarth church some feeling of its old importance and domination. It had control over the churches higher up the dale, churches much poorer than itself, a position which its vicars sometimes exploited to their own advantage."* (E.Pontefract & M.Hartley 1936). Inside the church there is a beautifully carved wooden screen and a reading desk made from two carved bench ends bearing the 'Rebus' of William de Heslington, Abbot of Jervaulx from 1472. These were carved by the famous Ripon Carvers in about 1506 and were originally housed at Jervaulx Abbey, coming to Aysgarth at the Dissolution of the Monasteries. There is an oak beam in the chancel with unusual carvings and the initials of the last Abbot of Jervaulx, Adam Sedbergh dated 1536. Close by is the curiously named Palmer Flatt Hotel, whose unusual name is a reminder of monastic days; the hotel stands on the site of a hospice for pilgrims.

BISHOPDALE is well known to many visitors because the main connecting road between Wharfedale and Wensleydale travels through the valley. The dale stretches six miles from the wild upper reaches at Kidstones Pass to the more placid surroundings at Aysgarth. After the last Ice Age Bishopdale was filled by a glacial lake which deposited silts on the land, this has given the dale particularly fertile soil *"The soil of Bishopdale produces the richest grass in the county, in some instances the land has let at £5 per acre."* (E.Bogg). This land has helped give Bishopdale a long and successful history of hunting and farming. During the Middle Ages the dale was the hunting preserve of the noblemen of Middleham Castle. Their ownership ended in the 17th century which gave the tenant farmers an opportunity to buy holdings and build their own houses; Bishopdale has some of the best examples of 17th century yeoman long houses in the Dales which are characterised by mullioned windows and carved door lintels (West New House dated 1635 is one of the finest). *"Here, scattered about the fell-sides and in the valley, are some of the finest and oldest of those stone built farmsteads for which the North-West Riding is so noted. Many of them are of great antiquity; some have histories attaching to them. At Thoralby, one of the most ancient villages hereabouts, the parish records of which go back to pre-Norman times, there is a farmstead which was originally a hunting-lodge of the great Barons of Rokeby."* (Fletcher 'Nooks and Corners of Yorkshire').

WEST BURTON is one of the loveliest villages in the Dales, indeed some claim it to be the most beautiful village in England. It is situated on the flanks of Naughtberry Hill, which divides Walden valley from Bishopdale, and is a peaceful almost secret place. This is because the main Bishopdale road by-passes the village and the road through the village and up into the Walden valley is a no through route. The village has an idyllic setting; wooded hills look down upon a surprisingly large village green, complete with a stone stepped obelisk (which dates from 1820) and stocks, surrounded by ancient stone cottages. This obelsik is not a market cross as West Burton has never had a market.

"But perhaps West Burton, at the foot of Waldendale, is the gem of all in Wensleydale, with school, stocks, and cross alongside the green, and the parish corn mill grinding away at the bottom next to the stream." (W.T.Palmer 'Odd corners in the Yorkshire Dales' 1937). At the lower end of the village a track leads past the old mill (now holiday homes) to Burton Force (also known as the Couldron Falls), set in a sylvan amphitheatre of rocks where Walden Beck tumbles over rock ledges. *"It was early autumn on our visit, and the branches of the trees and pale golden leaves were drooping feather-like over the rocks, outlined against the blue sky;*

through this leafy screen the crystal waters can be seen flowing towards the deep limestone scarr, over which it leaps with tumultuous sound, then whirling into eddies and a series of small falls, darts under the most picturesque of bridges thrown here and there across its waters, and as it courses along in merry career, past the creamy walls of Burton, carrying on its bosom the crisp autumn leaves, the overhanging trees stoop, as it were, to be kissed and reflected in the beautiful waters." (E.Bogg). The track which crosses Walden Beck near to the waterfall by way of a packhorse bridge forms part of the ancient packhorse route from West Burton to Middleham, known as Morpeth Gate; this can still be followed along a superb walled track. There is no church at West Burton hence the number of paths which lead to Aysgarth from the villages of Bishopdale. The Fox and Hounds overlooks the green (note the horse mounting blocks outside the pub), and is a typical Dales pub; functional yet comfortable with excellent local ale; to sit outside this pub on a warm summer's evening enjoying a glass of beer surrounded by such wonderful scenery is an experience not to be missed.

WEST BURTON TO KETTLEWELL

✦

"After visiting the isolated farm, I couldn't resist pulling my car off the unfenced road and climbing with my beagle, Dinah, to the high country which beckoned me. The snow had disappeared almost overnight leaving only runnels of white lying behind the walls and it was as though all the scents of the earth and growing things had been imprisoned and were released now by the spring sunshine in waves of a piercing sweetness. When I reached the summit I was breathless and gulped the crystal air greedily as though I could never get enough of it. Here there was no evidence of the hand of man and I walked with my dog among miles of heather, peat hags and bog pools with the black waters rippling and the tufts of rushes bending and swaying in the eternal wind. As the cloud shadows, racing on the wind, flew over me, trailing ribbons of shade and brightness over the endless browns and greens, I felt a rising exhilaration at being up there on the roof of Yorkshire. It was an empty landscape where no creature stirred and it was silent except for the cry of a distant bird, yet I felt a further surge of excitement in the solitude, a tingling sense of the nearness of all creation."

J.Herriot 'Every Living Thing' 1992.

WALK INFORMATION

Points of interest: The 'secret' valley, monastic and stagecoach routes, stones with strange powers, Brigante dikes and wild desolate moorland.

Distance:

West Burton to Horsehouse	5 miles
Horsehouse to Kettlewell	9 miles
Total	14 miles

Time: Allow 7 hours

Terrain: Most of this walk either follows unfenced surfaced roads or clear gravel/turf bridleways. Sections between West Burton and Cote Bridge, Horsehouse and Woodale follow riverside meadows. Excellent walking terrain all the way.

Ascent: 290 metres. Max. height 530 m.

Viewpoints: View from Fleensop Moor across Walden Valley.
Descent towards Horsehouse with views across Coverdale.
View of Kettlewell and Wharfedale from Top Mere Road

FACILITIES

ROUTE DESCRIPTION

(Map Twelve)

Leave West Burton along the road at the top of the village green (SP 'Walden only'). After only 1/4 mile take the FP to your left (SP 'Cote Bridge'), bear right across the field observing the FP sign and drop down to a FB over Walden Beck. After the FB take the path to the right (SP 'Cote Bridge'). Cross the field keeping to the field perimeter with the river on your right, through the gate to the right of the barn and head along the track down to Cote Bridge. Turn left and follow the metalled road for 1 mile, passing the turning for Whiterow Farm on your right and continue up the hill along the road then take the track (BW) to the left after the cattle grid. Follow the clear stony track up the side of the valley, then across the grassy summit to reach a gate. The track continues to the right across the moorland. After passing the turning to Fleensop Farm, drop down to cross a ford then continue along the stony track up the hill until the track joins a wall, head through the gate on your left. Follow the path bearing right across the grassy moorland until it joins a stone wall on your right. Go through the small wooden gate in the wall and head diagonally across the field (no clear path) to reach a gate in the bottom left hand corner and continue for a short distance until you reach a clear path. This path follows the line of the wall down the side of the hill. Cross over the wall stile (or gate) and follow the stony path down to Horsehouse

(Map Thirteen)

Turn right along the road, past the Thwaite Arms and out of the village. After 1/4 mile take the road to your left (SP 'Arkleside'), cross the bridge and turn right along the road. After crossing another bridge take the FP to the right (SP 'Woodale') through the gate. Head straight across the field then bear left at the SP to reach a wall gate which leads onto a farm track. Turn right along the track and continue straight ahead through a gate (past the farm on the right) to reach a small barn at the end of the track. The path continues to the right of this barn and crosses a field to reach a wall stile in the top left corner of the field, cross over the stream and up the other side then take the gate in the wall to the right (SP 'Braidley'). Cross the bridge over the River Cover, then turn left and follow the well marked path along the river bank. Forsake the path up to the right which leads to Braidley, and continue straight on following the river bank until you reach a gate which leads through a farmyard and into Woodale. Turn left along the metalled road heading up the dale and follow this unfenced road for approx. 3 miles, passing Cover Bridge, Coverhead Farm and Hunter's Stone.

(Map Fourteen)

At the head of the dale follow the clear green lane that branches away from the road diagonally to the right, marked with a SP, until you reach a gate. Continue through the gate and follow the very clear, stony path which skirts round the valley head following the SP's to Kettlewell. At the junction with the Starbotton path bear left (SP Kettlewell) and follow the green lane heading down towards Wharfedale. This green lane becomes a walled, stony lane (Top Mere Road) and then joins the metalled road which leads directly into Kettlewell.

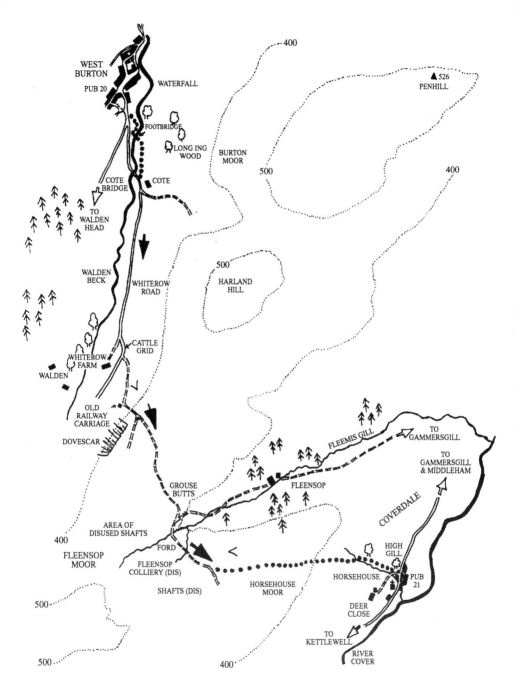

WEST BURTON
PUB 20
WATERFALL
FOOTBRIDGE
LONG ING WOOD
BURTON MOOR
400
▲526 PENHILL
500
400
COTE BRIDGE
COTE
TO WALDEN HEAD
WALDEN BECK
WHITEROW ROAD
HARLAND HILL
500
CATTLE GRID
WHITEROW FARM
WALDEN
OLD RAILWAY CARRIAGE
DOVESCAR
FLEEMIS GILL
TO GAMMERSGILL
TO GAMMERSGILL & MIDDLEHAM
GROUSE BUTTS
FLEENSOP
COVERDALE
AREA OF DISUSED SHAFTS
400
FLEENSOP MOOR
FORD
FLEENSOP COLLIERY (DIS)
SHAFTS (DIS)
HORSEHOUSE MOOR
HIGH GILL
HORSEHOUSE
PUB 21
500
DEER CLOSE
TO KETTLEWELL
RIVER COVER
500
400

MAP TWELVE

111

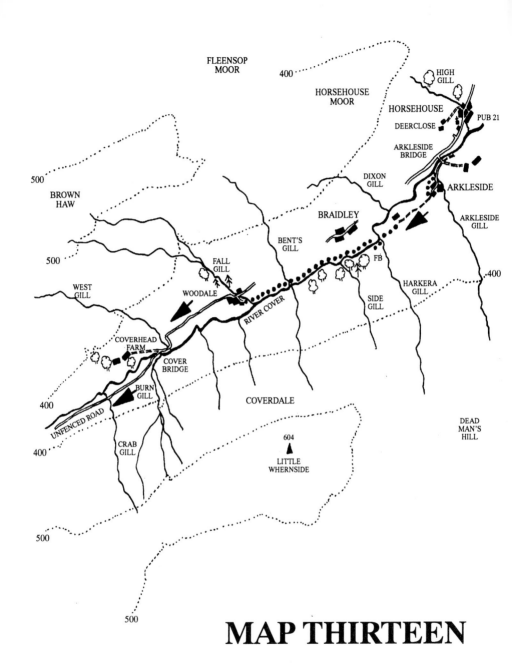

FLEENSOP MOOR

400

HORSEHOUSE MOOR

HIGH GILL

HORSEHOUSE

PUB 21

DEERCLOSE

ARKLESIDE BRIDGE

DIXON GILL

ARKLESIDE

500

BROWN HAW

BRAIDLEY

ARKLESIDE GILL

BENT'S GILL

500

FALL GILL

FB

WEST GILL

WOODALE

RIVER COVER

SIDE GILL

HARKERA GILL

400

COVERHEAD FARM

COVER BRIDGE

BURN GILL

COVERDALE

DEAD MAN'S HILL

400

UNFENCED ROAD

CRAB GILL

604

LITTLE WHERNSIDE

400

500

500

MAP THIRTEEN

MAP FOURTEEN

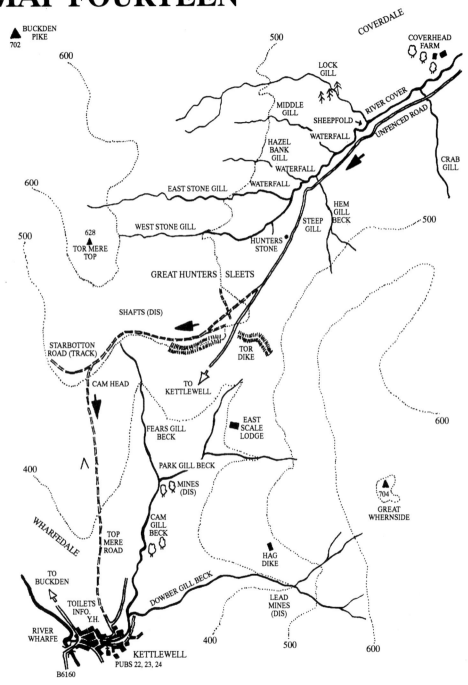

▲ BUCKDEN
PIKE
702

600

500

COVERDALE

COVERHEAD
FARM

LOCK
GILL

MIDDLE
GILL

SHEEPFOLD

RIVER COVER

UNFENCED ROAD

WATERFALL

HAZEL
BANK
GILL

WATERFALL

CRAB
GILL

600

EAST STONE GILL

WATERFALL

HEM
GILL
BECK

500

WEST STONE GILL

STEEP
GILL

500

628

HUNTERS
STONE

▲ TOR MERE
TOP

GREAT HUNTERS SLEETS

SHAFTS (DIS)

STARBOTTON
ROAD (TRACK)

TOR
DIKE

CAM HEAD

TO
KETTLEWELL

EAST
SCALE
LODGE

FEARS GILL
BECK

600

PARK GILL BECK

400

MINES
(DIS)

704

GREAT
WHERNSIDE

WHARFEDALE

TOP
MERE
ROAD

CAM
GILL
BECK

HAG
DIKE

TO
BUCKDEN

DOWBER GILL BECK

LEAD
MINES
(DIS)

TOILETS
INFO.
Y.H.

RIVER
WHARFE

400

500

600

KETTLEWELL
PUBS 22, 23, 24

B6160

THE VALLEY OF WALDEN (without a suffix-dale) is a hidden Dale, the last retreat of the Celtic tribes fleeing from the invading Norse and Anglo-Saxons, indeed 'Walden' may mean 'valley of the Welsh' as these native tribes were known. The beautiful steep sided valley with its scattering of farmsteads has changed little over the centuries; you would be forgiven if you thought that you had stepped back in time. Walden Beck is born on the flanks of Buckden Pike, which dominates the dale head, and only has a short journey before it meets Bishopdale Beck just beyond West Burton. Two minor roads lead into Walden from West Burton, however both are dead ends. *"The valley does not display its beauty all at once: round each twist and bend it gives a fresh delight....There is no suggestion of a main way about the road up it, which was made not for outsiders to travel through, but for the people of the dale."* (E.Pontefract & M.Hartley 'Wensleydale' 1936). These roads serve the farms at Walden Head (with the curiously named Kentucky House), and Dovescar. Ancient packhorse routes lead out of the dale; from Walden Head a track heads over Buckden Pike to Starbotton in Wharfedale, and another track begins at Whiterow Farm and goes over Fleensop Moor to Horsehouse in Coverdale. Both are superb tracks rewarding the walker with breathtaking views. *"I am particularly in love with the narrow track on the east side of Walden and it is one of Helen's favourite places. To drive up there, high above the tree-lined Walden Beck, is to escape easily from the workaday world. And if you leave your car and walk the old path over the moor till the fell tilts into Coverdale and the vast stream-furrowed face of Little Whernside rears up across the valley, you will be richly rewarded."* (J.Herriot 'James Herriot's Yorkshire' 1979). Fleensop Moor is littered with the remains of coal pits and lead mines; note the decaying ruins of an old stone built flue close to Cote Farm.

COVERDALE, from ancient British meaning a stream that flows through a deep ravine, stretches twelve miles from the isolated upper reaches of the dale where the River Cover is born on the flanks of Buckden Pike and Great Whernside, to the more gentle surroundings at Middleham. *"Its seclusion has resulted in much intermarrying, and it is not to be wondered at that superstition has kept a hold here, that old customs and beliefs which have their origin in pagan days survive."* (E.Pontefract & M.Hartley 1936). The area between Horsehouse and the dale head, referred to locally as High Dale, makes up some of the most wild, bleak and desolate country in England. *"Around us is an amphitheatre of wild hills and mountains, whose dark crests stand forth boldly against white breezy clouds which are sweeping hurriedly across the sky, their shadows climbing hill after hill like skeletons of some gigantic army."* (E.Bogg 'A Thousand Miles in Wharfedale' 1892). It is hard to imagine that the road which winds its way precariously up the dale was once an important monastic and packhorse route, but most amazingly the section between Middleham and Kettlewell formed part of the London to Richmond stage coach route. The very steep Park Rash Pass between the dale head and Kettlewell, with its hair-pin bend, was considered too dangerous and the route was altered. *"High up yonder, between Great Whernside and Buckden Pike, on the south and west, and Pen Hill on the north, the little River Cover has its birth, oozing out of the dark waste of moorland, which even to-day, is a vast solitude of unreclaimed land. Here during the thousand years of changeful destiny, from the incoming of the Roman to the Conquest of the Norman, this neck of land, was the scene of many fierce and sanguinary struggles. Other and more picturesque scenes, have no doubt, been often witnessed along this mountain road, cavalcades of knights, princes and prelates, and their numerous attendants; the Nevilles of Middleham and Raby; that celebrated figure of Warwick, the King-maker, and a host of others, who have left their names on the historic scroll, have passed and repassed over this wild mountain track to Middleham, Richmond, Raby, Brancepeth, etc."* (E.Bogg 'Beautiful Wensleydale' 1925).

Place names in the dale are derived mainly from Norse for example Caldbergh, Scrafton, Swineside, Arkleside, Gammersgill; these villages were originally clearings in the forest that once covered Coverdale. Carlton acted as the forest headquarters and it is reputed that courts of the forest were held there; the village was also the home of Henry Constantine, a 19th century local dialect poet. Caldbergh has literary connections as the birthplace of Miles Coverdale who first translated the Bible into English in 1535.

Between Carlton and Middleham stands Coverham Abbey which was built in 1212 and housed an Abbot and sixteen Canons. For many centuries the abbey provided welcome accommodation for travellers and employment for local people, however this ended with the Dissolution of the Monasteries. Very little remains of the abbey today largely due to the stone being plundered to build houses. *"The spirits of the monks seem still to hover around the ruined walls; they were lovers of beautiful nature, and chose their dwelling places with an artist's and a poet's eye. Though centuries have passsed since they were driven forth, and their homes despoiled, yet their memory still lingers, and the charms of nature, art, and peaceful solitude which soothed their spirits still seem to cling around as we stand and muse within the ruined sanctuary."* (E.Bogg 'From Eden Vale to the Plains of York'). Guarding the entrance to Coverdale stands the majestic Middleham Castle, the 'Windsor of the North'. This castle dates from Norman times and was the stronghold of the powerful Neville family for many years. Richard III spent several years at Middleham where he met his wife Lady Anne Neville and their son Edward, Prince of Wales, was born. The castle fell into disrepair after Richard III was killed at the Battle of Bosworth in 1485, but remained Crown property until 1625 when it passed into private ownership. Today Middleham is a centre for racehorse training, the grassy moors in the area provide perfect gallops.

Dead Man's Hill was the scene of a terrible murder in 1728, when a local innkeeper killed three Scottish pedlars and buried their headless bodies on the moor, *"It was noticed too that the people at the inn seemed prosperous, and that many of the farmers in the district were using Scotch ponies and their wives wearing Paisley shawls. A search was made, and the bodies of the victims, all headless, were found buried near the house."* (E.Pontefract & M.Hartley 1936).

HORSEHOUSE *"... was famous in olden days, when packhorse trains left Knaresborough and there was open travel, not a wall to cross, a gate to open all the way to Scotland."* (W.T.Palmer 'Odd Corners in the Yorkshire Dales' 1937). Horsehouse developed as an overnight stop for packhorses and stage coaches (hence the name) with two inns to quench the thirst of the tired travellers. The Thwaite Arms, with its small rooms and stone flagged floors, still refreshes weary travellers, however the other inn, known as the Kings Head, closed many years ago. *"A house high above the road was the other (inn); it has a long stone porch at the back of it where the men placed the food, and a hole in the*

garden, now partly filled in, was the dog pit where drovers' dogs were put for the night." (E.Pontefract & M.Hartley 1936). St Botolph's Church dates from the 15th century when it was serviced by the monks of Coverham Abbey. The present building was extensively 'renovated' in 1869.

HIGH DALE is the name given to the wild upper reaches of Coverdale, *"The general characteristic of the dale is bleakness."* (Fletcher 'Nooks and Corners of Yorkshire') there is, however, beauty in such wilderness *"...we look up the vale to Great Whernside, and through the autumn mists which lie along the vale we can see Little Whernside on the left, and on the right the heights of Buckden Pike, waves of sunlight tinge with golden the mighty billows of gloomy, purple moors."* (E.Bogg). The hamlets of the upper dale (Arkleside, Braidley, Woodale and Coverheads) are small farming communities and have been for centuries. The ground rises steadily for six miles from Horsehouse to the dale head where the road reaches a height of 503 metres; Great Whernside (704 m) and Buckden Pike (702 m) stand guard over the pass into Wharfedale. Near the highest point on the road stands Hunter's Stone (inscribed with a cross) which was placed there by the monks of Coverham to help guide them over the moorland. This stone reputedly possesses strange powers; when the clock strikes twelve at Hunter's Hall (otherwise known as Coverhead Farm which stands on the site of a hunting hall which belonged to the Lords of Middleham) the stone spins round.

The monastic route did not follow the now metalled road down to Kettlewell via Park Rash but branched off across the moors to drop down into Kettlewell by way of Top Mere Road; this superb walled green lane affords breathtaking views of Wharfedale. *"It is said that the scenery and contour of the mountains around Kettlewell are nearly a fac-simile of the Valley of Jehosaphat, in Palestine."* (E.Bogg 1892). Tor Dike stretches for over a mile along the ridge which divides Wharfedale from

Coverdale. This impressive defensive ditch was built c.AD 70 by the Brigantes to prevent a Roman invasion of the northern dales. It formed part of a system which included the ditches and ramparts near Grinton in Swaledale and the forts on Ingleborough and Addleborough. *"Legend says, this place was formerly the habitation of spirits supposed to have been ghosts of slain warriors hovering around the battleground."* (E.Bogg 1892). Unfortunately these defenses were not enough to stop the Romans. We now sadly leave Coverdale to return to Wharfedale, *"As we leave Leyburn we get a most beautiful view up Coverdale, with the two Whernsides standing out most conspicuously at the head of the valley, and it is this last view of Coverdale, and the great valley from which it branches, that remains in the mind as one of the finest pictures of this most remarkable portion of Yorkshire."* (G.Home 'Yorkshire' 1908).

KETTLEWELL (named after Ketel, a Norse-Irish chieftain) originally began as a Norse settlement, but only really grew in importance from the 12th century onwards when part of the manor of Kettlewell was granted to the monks of Coverham Abbey, the other half being held by the Nevilles of Middleham.

A market charter was granted in the 13th century and this, combined with its monastic connections and location (the Roman road from Ilkley to Bainbridge came through Kettlewell, as did the monastic route from Coverham Abbey, numerous packhorse routes and the stage coach route from London), made Kettlewell a thriving community. At one time the village supported thirteen inns that helped quench the thirst of the miners, travellers and market-goers.

Following the Dissolution of the Monasteries and the Rising of the North in the 16th century, which led to the sequestration of the Neville's lands, the manor became Crown property. In 1656 it was sold to a group of local men who became the Trust Lords of Kettlewell. These Trust Lords were elected from the freeholders to ensure that the manorial dues and rights were kept in trust. *"The result of this was that there grew up here a community of important yeomen, taking part in the life of the district, and giving a certain amount of affluence to it."* (E.Pontefract & M.Hartley 'Wharfedale' 1938). The Trust Lords of Kettlewell still draw income from land that they own and use the money for improvements in the village. Lead mining and textiles in the 18th and 19th centuries brought new prosperity to Kettlewell; most of the houses in the village date from this period, although a handful of 17th century houses remain. Behind the village can be seen the remains of a smelting mill which was used from 1700 to 1886. The Church of St Mary dates back to Norman times, however it was demolished in 1882 and a new Victorian church built. Only the Norman font is original complete with a carving of a boar's head, the badge of the Neville's. The church does have many notable features including a framed document dating from 1380 concerning the monks of Coverham Abbey as well as unusual stained glass depicting the Battle of the Somme - look out for the gravestone of a man who died in 1770 at the ripe old age of 117! More recently Kettlewell has become popular with walkers, its lovely setting and the numerous paths which radiate in every direction make it an ideal tourist centre. *"But one can easily mark the change coming over the scene; the screech of the railway engine is gradually drawing nearer, and many are the aliens seeking to obtain a foothold in this isolated dale within a dale. The electric light is already an installed fact - here as well as Grassington."* (E.Bogg 'By the Banks of the Wharfe' 1921). There are three good inns to choose from; the Racehorses Hotel (which dates from 1740), the King's Head (complete with inglenook fireplace) and the Blue Bell, names reminiscent of the long forgotten stagecoaching era and nothing to do with racing and flowers as you may have thought. *"Its comfortable little inns make Kettlewell a very fine centre for rambles in the wild dales that run up towards the head of Wharfedale."* (G.Home 1908). It is worth spending time exploring the alleys and lanes that make up Kettlewell to discover it's three inns, shops, youth hostel, Post Office, Cafes, church, maypole and the beck which runs through it plus lots more. Kettlewell feels more like a town than a village.

John A. Ives, 199.

· ·

KETTLEWELL TO GRASSINGTON

✦

"The Yorkshire highlands, raking up to wide-flung mountain fastnesses, lie remote from usual haunts; and their people are rooted in free, unspoiled acres. There is only the one road to knowledge of the Dales and Dalesfolk -lifelong intimacy with the rugged scarps, the hidden glens, the homesteads, big and little, perched on the mountains' feet or gathered into grey, comely villages. Here and there a market town is busy with agriculture's pleasant merchandise. Never are men far from the overwatching moors, whose minstrels are the plover and curlew, grouse and hoarse hoodie-crow. Land and people have grown into a sure, ripe communion, and to be admitted to their fellowship is to learn the deeper things that reach the true romance. Legend and history mingle with the everyday of human intercourse. Storm and shine, the nor'-easter's bite on sleety uplands, the fragrance of swathed hayfields when summer dusks steal down about a land of plenty, the gypsies' caravans, slow-winding through a country friendly to them from the ancient days -who shall tell what goes to the Dales' full glamour?"

H. Sutcliffe 'The Striding Dales' 1929.

WALK INFORMATION

Points of interest: Ancient 'green lanes', deserted long-houses, numerous abandoned lead mines, the hidden village of the cobblers, '101 ways to cross a stream' and the powerful force of Linton Falls.

Distance:
Kettlewell to Hebden	9 miles
Hebden to Grassington	3 miles
Total	12 miles

Time: Allow 6 hours

Terrain: Section from Kettlewell to Hebden along well defined moorland paths and tracks, can be extremely exposed.
Section from Hebden to Grassington follows clear paths across meadowland and along quiet country lanes.

Ascent: 302 metres. Max. height 512 m.

Viewpoints: Ascent from Kettlewell to Conistone Moor affords good views of Upper Wharfedale. Extensive views from Capplestone Gate. Waterfalls at Linton.

FACILITIES

Kettlewell	Inn / B&B / Shop / P.O. / Cafe / Bus / Phone / Toilets / Info
Hebden	Inn / B&B / Shop / P.O. / Cafe / Bus / Phone / Toilets / Info
Thorpe	B&B
Linton	Inn / B&B / Bus / Phone / Toilets
Grassington	Inn / B&B / Shop / P.O. / Cafe / Bus / Phone / Toilets / Info

ROUTE DESCRIPTION

(Map fifteen)

Leave Kettlewell via the road to the right of the stream near to the 'King's Head' pub. After you have left the houses behind, follow the track up to the right (SP 'Whernside Pasture'). This steep track winds up the hillside through three gates and is clearly signposted (the last gate is up to the left). After the third gate the path levels out and divides into several tracks; take the right FP keeping close to the stone wall. Follow this wall for 1/4 mile then bear left away from the wall to reach the stile directly ahead. Cross this wooden stile then continue across the field, bearing slightly to the left, to reach a stone wall stile then across the next field to reach a second stone stile. The path now becomes clearer (SP) and continues along a grassy track to the left of the small ridge to reach a stile. Continue along the clear path over more wall stiles (keep left of the limestone outcrop and the right angle in the wall), and head up across the rough field (ignore the gate up to the left on the ridge) to reach a wall stile (SP), after which bear up to the left to a stile (SP) which brings you out into an area of mining debris and spoil heaps. At the three finger SP take the right hand path which heads through the spoil heaps and then left following the line of the wall (yellow markers) to reach a stile near to a white trig point (Capplestone Gate). Cross the stile and follow the clear track down the hillside (Conistone Turf Road), past a conifer plantation then turn left to reach a farm track (Bycliffe Road). Head right (SP Conistone) along the track, passing through an area of limestone pavements until you reach a FP on your left (SP 'Grassington Dalesway'). Head left along this FP until you reach a stone wall. After the wall take the path which branches up to the left (not signposted) to reach a wall gate. After the gate cross the wall stile to the right, then head diagonally left up the hillside to reach the far left hand corner of the field near to a small wood. Continue along the path passing to the left of the wood, keeping close to the wall. Leave the wall after a while and follow the clear path up the hill to reach the deserted Bare House Farm.

(Map sixteen)

Keep the farm and its small enclosure to your right, and join a clear farm track after passing a barn (marked by a SP). Head right along this track for approx. 1 mile until you reach the Grassington road at Yarnbury. Turn right along the road then take the track opposite the house heading through the old lead mining area (SP 'Hebden'). Where the track divides (chimney in distance) follow the right hand branch past spoil heaps and continue straight ahead to reach a gate. The path continues to the left (SP) twisting down hill to reach Hebden Beck. Turn right and follow the path next to the stream for approx. 1 mile until you reach a road and some cottages at Hole Bottom, continue along the road into the centre of Hebden. Cross the main road and go straight ahead (SP 'Burnsall') passing the shop on your right and continue out of the village along the road. After the houses have been left behind take the wall gate to your right (SP) and cross the suspension bridge over the Wharfe. After the bridge turn left then almost immediately right straight up the hill (BW 'Thorpe') to reach the main road, cross this road and follow the lane opposite into Thorpe and continue to follow this road out of the village bearing right. Immediately after leaving Thorpe take the left fork in the road and follow this for approx 1/2 mile (ignore first FP to right 'BW to B6160') and take the FP to the right (SP 'Linton') near a ruined barn. Follow the clear path straight ahead across fields to join a farm track that leads through a farmyard and into Linton. Head right out of Linton along the main road towards Grassington, go straight on at the crossroads with the B6160 then take the road to the right before the bridge towards Linton Church (SP). Follow the FP to Linton Falls to the left of the houses, (the path skirts to the right behind the houses forsaking the packhorse bridge), cross the bridge over the falls and follow the path directly ahead into Grassington car park.

MAP FIFTEEN

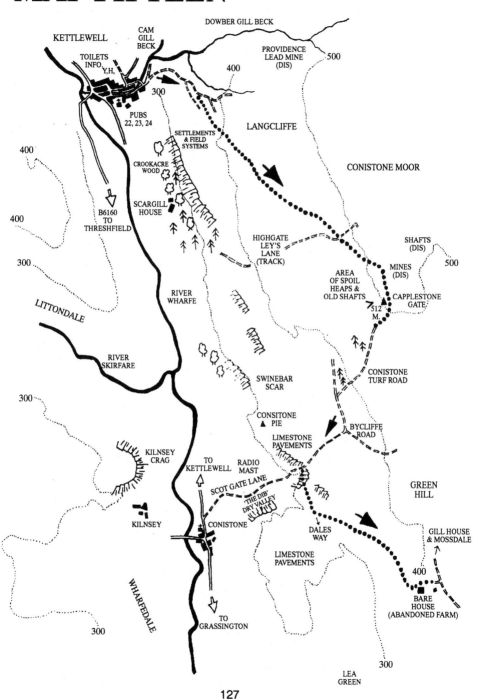

MAP SIXTEEN

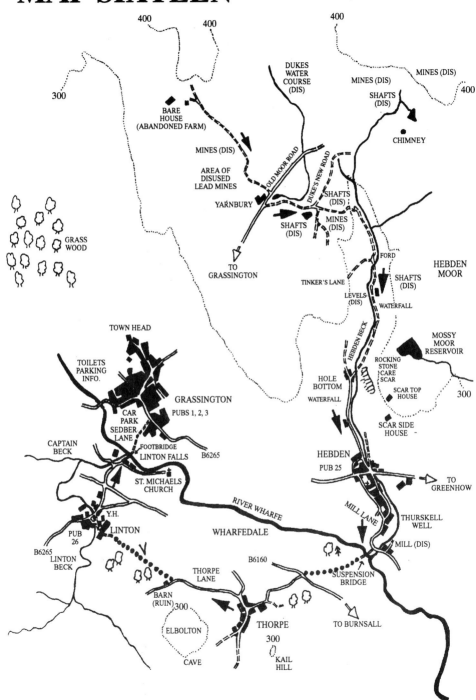

400   400   400

DUKES
WATER
COURSE
(DIS)

MINES (DIS)   MINES (DIS)

300

BARE
HOUSE
(ABANDONED FARM)

SHAFTS
(DIS)

400

CHIMNEY

MINES (DIS)

AREA OF
DISUSED
LEAD MINES

OLD MOOR ROAD

DUKE'S NEW ROAD

YARNBURY

SHAFTS
(DIS)

SHAFTS
(DIS)

MINES
(DIS)

HEBDEN
MOOR

TO
GRASSINGTON

GRASS
WOOD

TINKER'S LANE

LEVELS
(DIS)

FORD

SHAFTS
(DIS)

WATERFALL

TOWN HEAD

HEBDEN BECK

MOSSY
MOOR
RESERVOIR

TOILETS
PARKING
INFO.

GRASSINGTON

PUBS 1, 2, 3

HOLE
BOTTOM

WATERFALL

ROCKING
STONE
CARE
SCAR

SCAR TOP
HOUSE

300

CAR
PARK
SEDBER
LANE

CAPTAIN
BECK

FOOTBRIDGE
LINTON FALLS

ST. MICHAELS
CHURCH

B6265

SCAR SIDE
HOUSE

HEBDEN

PUB 25

TO
GREENHOW

Y.H.

PUB
26

LINTON

RIVER WHARFE

MILL LANE

THURSKELL
WELL

B6265

LINTON
BECK

WHARFEDALE

MILL (DIS)

THORPE
LANE

B6160

SUSPENSION
BRIDGE

BARN
(RUIN) 300

ELBOLTON

THORPE

300

TO BURNSALL

CAVE

KAIL
HILL

CONISTONE MOOR is criss-crossed by old packhorse routes as well as more modern long distance walks. This is because Conistone has been an important crossing point of the Wharfe for centuries; Conistone Bridge was originally constructed in monastic times as part of the route from Fountains Abbey to the grazing lands in the Lake District via Mastiles Lane. Bycliffe Road is a superb green lane which climbs over Conistone Moor to reach Middlesmoor in Nidderdale. The Conistone Turf Road links Conistone with the lower slopes of Great Whernside where peat was once cut, dried and then used as fuel in the houses of Upper Wharfedale. *"These paths are nearly as old as the hills and have been trod for centuries, and are the heritage of every free-born Briton."* (E.Bogg 'By the Banks of the Wharfe' 1921). The 84 mile 'Dales Way' also crosses Conistone Moor on its way from Ilkley to Bowness-on-Windermere.

The panorama from Capplestone Gate is extensive with views over Wharfedale and beyond to Pendle Hill, Pen-y-Ghent, Fountains Fell, Yockenthwaite Moor and Buckden Pike. High on the fell side, near to Yarnbury, stands the deserted farm of Bare House (also known as Barras). The name is derived from the Norse 'bargh-hus' meaning 'hill farm' as the early Norse settlers chose isolated moorland locations for their farms. The monks from Fountains Abbey had a farm here, although following the Dissolution of the Monasteries the tenant farmer would have been able to purchase the property. These farmers became relatively affluent and subsequently the farm was rebuilt in 1620. Bare House is a good example of a long house with living accommodation and barn all under the same roof. The walled lane from Yarnbury to Bare House (known as Lime Kiln Lane) affords good views of these wind swept uplands. *"Follow this rough cart-road until you reach a gate which leads to the moor. Pass through, and pause a few moments to view the landscape, which at this point is superb- a very Kaleidoscope of contrasts under the changing conditions of sun and cloud overhead. On the right you have a view of the treeless valley of Mossdale, with Whernside in the background. On the left you see, a field or two away, Barras."* (J.Crowther 'Rambles Round Grassington' 1920).

Lime Kiln Lane continues past Bare House across the moors to eventually reach Gill House, one of the most solitary farmhouses in the Dales, now sadly uninhabited. *"In a clump of trees to the right is the lonely farm of Gill House, where the inhabitants often wake up on a winters morning to find the snow up to their bedroom windows."* (E.Pontefract & M.Hartley 'Wharfedale' 1938). Beyond Gill House there is nothing but bleak, wild, unenclosed moorland for several miles before dropping down into Nidderdale.

YARNBURY was the home of the mining manager and the administrative centre for the lead mining which once took place on the surrounding moorland. This area is littered with the remains of the lead mining industry which flourished during the 18th and 19th centuries, although lead has been mined in this area since Roman times. The earliest shafts were bell pits dating mainly from the 17th century, however as technology improved during the late 18th century deeper shafts were constructed. The improved productivity meant that larger furnaces had to be built, better drainage of the shafts was required and water power was needed. This resulted in the construction of the Duke's Watercourse (named after the Dukes of Devonshire who owned the land and developed the mines) which provided water to the mining field from dams by way of a canal system that stretched for six miles. The Cupola smelt mill chimney and associated flue system was built to improve the efficiency of the smelt mill and help disperse the poisonous fumes; the chimney stands 60 feet high and is an unmistakable landmark for miles around. *"The* lead mines, from what one sees during this walk, covered a large area. They had good buildings, and must have employed a large number of workpeople. Special attention appears to have been given to the making of levels to drain the water from the mines on the moors during mining operations some 60 years ago." (J.Crowther 1920). The numerous shafts, spoil heaps and ruinous buildings stand as a silent tribute to the men who once worked in these inhospitable uplands. *"Occasionally a faint knocking sound is heard in old mines. The miners believed that this was made by the ghosts of men killed in the mines, and that it came as a warning of an accident. They would leave off work for the day if they heard the 'knockers'."* (E.Pontefract & M.Hartley 1938). Extreme care must be taken when exploring this area.

HEBDEN GILL leads down from the moors to the village of Hebden. The Gill is steep sided and narrow with the fast flowing Hebden Beck competing with the old miners' track for space along the valley floor. Again there are relics of the lead mining industry all around. *"Away upwards, we climb under the shadow of immense rock; the large mass which peers over the valley is named the Rocking Stone, and can be moved, the natives say, by a slight pressure. Upwards still, the mines are reached; curious old holes and shafts are to be seen near the torrent, which at this place flows over a shelf of rock. Still upwards, all signs of humanity are left behind, and we tread the wild, wild moorland; even the stone walls which spoil many a rugged landscape are left."* (E.Bogg 'A Thousand Miles in Wharfedale' 1892). Beyond Hole Bottom, just out of sight from the road, is a waterfall known as Scala Force which has a beautiful setting in a wooded gorge.

HEBDEN *"Its glory is its setting by a deep wooded glen, where the Hebden Beck comes from a pretty waterfall on its way to the Wharfe. There are two bridges side by side, the big one carrying the moorland road. The old houses and the century-old church look up to the enfolding hills, and from the rocky crags across the stream is a* *wonderful panorama of mountain scenery."* (A.Mee 'Yorkshire West Riding' 1941). Hebden was originally a small village centred around the old turnpike bridge which crosses Hebden Beck, some of the houses in this part of Hebden date from the 17th century. The real growth period began in the early 19th century as more people came to the area to seek work in the lead mining industry. Most of the village dates from this period including the replacement bridge (1827), the church (1841) and the school (1875) as well as numerous miners' cottages, *"Lead mining, which formerly gave employment to many of the people, having now become unprofitable, has been the cause of the decrease of the inhabitants - hence the reason of the many tenantless houses in the village."* (E.Bogg 1892).

Hebden Mill helped provide work producing cotton products after the mines closed. The mill closed in 1937 and has been converted for residential use. Thurskell Well is a rare example of a well which still retains its pagan god dedication (Thor) dating back to Norse times; most wells have been Christianized over the centuries, *"Here people assembled to worship and partake of the water, as communicants, to-day, do of wine."* (E.Bogg 1921). *"One can imagine that the strangeness of life-giving water coming apparently from nowhere through a rock or mossy patch in the hillside would, to primitive people with their eye for essential truth, seem like a miracle - an appearance of something divine. So the custom of 'well-dressings', and the joyous festival in connection with them, go back to prehistoric times. Thruskell is famed for its gushing water and also for having kept its original name, the fountain of Thor."* (C.E.Lewis 'Wharfedale'). I recommend the excellent Timothy Taylor's beers at the Clarendon Hotel to quench your thirst rather than the well water.

THORPE lies hidden between the hills of Elbolton and Kail and is not visible from any part of Wharfedale; your first view of the village is when you are actually entering it. *"The first view of the place is astonishing; approach by whatever side you will* *it is so completely hidden by surrounding fells, over whose solitary wastes the eye is ranging, when, like a dream or oasis in the desert, this old time village spreads before us."* (E.Bogg 1892). The bright green hills which help conceal Thorpe are known as the Reef Knolls, whose underlying rocks are limestone with a high coral and shell content - these rocks would have started life as coral reefs in a warm shallow sea millions of years ago. *"On the summit of the hill called Elbolton, high above the little village of Thorpe, evidence has been found of sunworship being practised there. Even to this day there is, amongst the older folk of the district, a certain amount of belief in fairies and ghosts, and places are pointed out on the hillsides where they are said to dance."* (Fletcher 'Nooks and Corners of Yorkshire').

For such a small place Thorpe has a fascinating history. The village was a safe haven for people of the dale against Scottish raiders during the 14th and 15th centuries. Thorpe was also reputedly the home of very highly skilled shoemakers who first started making shoes for the monks of Fountains Abbey. *"After the Abbeys were dissolved the shoemakers went on working in Thorpe - at one time there were forty of them - and it became famous for its fine shoes. People would travel long distances to get a pair fitted and made here. An old woman who died only a few years ago used to tell how she rode over from Grassington as a young woman to be measured for shoes at Thorpe. Her father was a Grassington shoemaker himself, but she said there were no shoes like Thorpe shoes. As late as 1822 there were two shoemakers and one bootmaker at Thorpe. The last of the old craftsmen, Kit Inman, died two years ago at Burnsall, and there is not even a cobbler now."* (M.Hartley & E.Pontefract 1938).

Knave Knoll Hole (known locally as Navvy Noddle Hole) is a cave which is situated on the west side of Elbolton Hill in which human remains dating back 2-3,000 years were discovered alongside Arctic animals including wolves, bears and reindeer; a reminder of the Dales landscape after the last Ice Age. *"Above the village is Elbolton Hill 1100 feet high, with a cave where extinct animals once sheltered, and where the bones of 12 men sitting in a ring were found 20 centuries after they had died."* (A. Mee 1941).

LINTON is a good example of an Anglian settlement with stone houses facing onto a large green. Linton Beck, which flows through the village, is crossed by a variety of bridges, including a road bridge, clapper bridge, packhorse bridge, stepping stones and fords; *"Perhaps there is some magical significance in crossing the water."* (N.Duerden 'Portrait of the Dales' 1978). *"Linton ...is a charmingly characteristic Craven village, its dwellings clustered pleasantly around the green. A stream barely deep enough to cover its pebbles, ripples and wimples through the centre of the spacious 'green'; yet this same stream at flood is so forceful as to formerly make crossing it dangerous to man or beast."* (E.Bogg 1921). It is easy to understand why the village was voted 'Loveliest in the North' by the News Chronicle in 1949 as the beck, packhorse bridge, green and old houses including a classic Dales' inn create an attractive scene.

Dominating the village is the Fountaine Hospital which was founded and endowed in 1721 by the will of Richard Fountaine to provide almshouses for six poor people of the parish. Richard Fountaine was a local man who made his fortune as a coffin maker in London during the Great Plague! The Fountaine Trust continues to draw income for the almshouses from land it owns in the area. The building was designed by Sir John Vanbrugh, who also designed Castle Howard, and introduced the Classical style of building to the Dales. *"There is a maypole on the green, and at one end are the imposing almshouses founded in the 18th century and enlarged in the 19th, looking like a little town hall with their domed tower."* (A.Mee 1941). Other notable buildings in the village are the Old Hall which dates from the 17th century with Georgian extensions, White Abbey is a fine example of a 17th century yeoman's house and was also the home of the famous Dales author Halliwell Sutcliffe. A small glacial lake once filled the flat fields behind the village, these marshy conditions were ideal for the growing of flax from which linen was made, indeed the name Linton is probably derived from the Anglo-Saxon 'lin' meaning flax and 'tun' meaning enclosure. Flax was last grown in the early 19th century and sadly the lake was drained around 1850. *"The tarn has gone now, and no flax waves here, and the valley seems to wait and listen pathetically, as if it wished the old busy times back again."* (E.Pontefract & M.Hartley 1938). Note the Arthur Anderton Memorial Institute and Men's Reading Room situated alongside the road between Linton and the Falls - obviously built in the days before educational enlightenment.

Linton Church, dedicated to St Michael and All Angels, can be found half a mile from the village close to the Wharfe and serves the villages of Linton, Grassington, Hebden and Threshfield as it has done for centuries; a path leads from each village to the church. It is an ancient building dating from the 12th century with many original Norman features, although much modification took place in the 14th and 15th centuries. It is built in characteristic Dales style - long and low with a bell turret rather than a tower to call the faithful. Linton Falls make an impressive end to this walk, as the Wharfe tumbles spectacularly over rocks caused by the Craven Fault (which also account for Malham Cove), *"At flood time the Wharfe at Linton 'falls', in its wild impetuous rush, is hurled over the obstructive rocks that make the 'rapids' with thunderous roar, the grey clouds of spray and foam flung forth adds a feeling of awe to the weird effect."* (E.Bogg 1921). Beside the falls Linton Mill once ground corn, spun worsteds and then cotton until it closed in 1959. The mill has been rebuilt as houses.

"I walked along the busy streets to the station, aware of my curious glances, for my clothes were unkempt and dirty, and my shoes, with heels gone and soles barely holding on, were so fast falling to pieces that I had to slide my feet as I walked lest they fall completely asunder. I was a spectre from a midden, but I marched in triumph...Respectability is often regarded as a matter of starch; hill-wandering takes all the starch out of a man, first out of his clothes, then out of his soul. And note, this cleansing process does not leave him limp, but gives him strength and a new vision."

A Wainwright 'A Pennine Journey -
The Story of a Long Walk in 1938'.

The End.

THE COUNTRY CODE

✦

Enjoy the countryside and respect its life and work

Keep dogs under control

Keep to public rights of way

Use stiles and gates to cross boundaries

Take litter home

Do not touch crops, machinery or livestock

Protect fauna and flora

Do not make excessive noise

Close gates behind you

Guard against risk of fire

Take care on country roads

Safeguard water supplies

BIBLIOGRAPHY

The following books are listed as follows: author, title, date first published and publisher.

T. Shaw, 'The History of Wharfedale', 1830, William Walker.

E. Bogg, 'A Thousand Miles in Wharfedale', 1892, Goodall & Suddick.

W. Andrews, 'Bygone Yorkshire', 1892, A Brown & Sons.

A.H. Norway, 'Highways and Byways in Yorkshire', 1899, Macmillan General Books.

G. Home, 'Yorkshire', 1908, A & C Black Ltd.

J. Crowther, 'Rambles Round Grassington', 1920, T A J Waddington.

E. Bogg, 'By the Banks of the Wharfe', 1921, J Miles (Rhodes & Sons Ltd, Printers).

E. Bogg, 'The Middle Valley of the Wharfe', 1922, J Miles (Rhodes & Sons Ltd, Printers).

E. Bogg, 'Beautiful Wensleydale and By the Banks of the Yore', 1925, J Miles, (Rhodes & Sons Ltd, Printers).

H. Sutcliffe, 'The Striding Dales', 1929, F Warne & Co Ltd.

E. Pontefract & M. Hartley, 'Swaledale', 1934, Smith Settle.

E. Pontefract & M. Hartley, 'Wensleydale', 1936, Smith Settle.

W. T. Palmer, 'Odd Corners in the Yorkshire Dales', 1937,
Skeffington & Sons Ltd.

E. Pontefract & M. Hartley, 'Wharfedale', 1938,
Smith Settle.

E. Pontefract & M. Hartley, 'Yorkshire Tour', 1939,
J M Dent & Sons Ltd.

A. Mee, 'Yorkshire North Riding', 1941,
Hodder & Stoughton Ltd.

A. Mee, 'Yorkshire West Riding', 1941,
Hodder & Stoughton Ltd.

G. B. Wood, 'Yorkshire Tribute', 1950, Methuen.

Various, 'The Dalesman', Vols 14-21 1952 - 1960,
Dalesman .Publishing.

J. & R. Fairfax- Blakeborough, 'The Spirit of Yorkshire', 1954,
B. T. Batsford Ltd.

M. Hartley & J. Ingliby, 'The Wonders of Yorkshire', 1959,
J. M. Dent & Sons Ltd.

A. Raistrick & J. Illingworth,
'The Face of North-West Yorkshire', 1967,
Dalesman Publishing.

J. Hammond, 'Complete Yorkshire', 1973,
Ward Lock Ltd.

I. Dewhirst, 'Yorkshire Through the Years', 1975,
B. T. Batsford Ltd.

R. A. Carter, 'Yorkshire Churches', 1976, Watmoughs.

G. Wright, 'The Yorkshire Dales', 1977,
David & Charles.

N. Wingate & L. L. Stafford,
'Grassington and Wharfedale', 1977,
Wingate & Stafford.

N. Duerden, 'Portrait of the Dales', 1978,
R. Hale Ltd.

J. Herriot, 'James Herriot's Yorkshire', 1979,
Michael Joseph.

Ordnance Survey/AA, 'Leisure Guide Yorkshire Dales, 1985,
AA/OS.

A. Wainwright, 'Wainwright on the Pennine Way',1985,
Michael Joseph.

F. Duerden, 'Great Walks Yorkshire Dales', 1986,
Ward Lock Ltd.

A. Wainwright, 'A Pennine Journey - The Story of
a Long Walk in 1938', 1986,
Michael Joseph.(pp11,16-17,29,30-31,36,41-42,213)
Reproduced by permission of Penguin Books Ltd.

M. Harding, 'Walking the Dales', 1986, Michael Joseph.

G. White, 'Walks in Swaledale', 1986, Dalesman.

J. Hillaby, 'John Hillaby's Yorkshire', 1986, Constable.

K. Piggin, 'Swaledale & Wensleydale', 1987,
Jarrold & Sons Ltd.

Ordnance Survey, 'The Yorkshire Dales and York', 1989,
OS/Jarrold Publications.

B. Pepper, 'A Haunt of Rare Souls
- The Old Inns and Pubs of Yorkshire', 1990,
Smith Settle.

R. Thompson, 'North Yorkshire Ale', 1991, CAMRA.

J. Morrison, 'The Real Wensleydale', 1991, CP Printing.

D. Gerrard, 'The Real Swaledale', 1991, CP Printing.

W. R. Mitchell, 'High Dale Country', 1991, Souvenir Press.

A. Wainwright, 'Wainwright in the Limestone Dales', 1991,
Michael Joseph.
Reproduced by permission of Penguin Books Ltd.

J. Herriot, 'Every Living Thing', 1992, Michael Joseph.

Various, 'The Dalesman', 1975, 1986, 1988, 1990, 1993, 1994,
Dalesman Publishing.

W. Andrews, 'Picturesque Yorkshire', date unknown,
Valentine & Sons Ltd.

Fletcher, 'Nooks & Corners of Yorkshire', date unknown,
Nash.
C. E. Lewis, 'Wharfedale', date unknown, S P C K.

E. Bogg, 'From Eden Vale to the Plains of York',
date unknown, Goodall & Suddick.

THE INN WAY ...*to the Yorkshire Dales*
LOG BOOK

"Drinking in the scenery"

◆

Make sure you visit all 26 inns along the way. Fill in your Log Book by using the 'clippers' which can be found attached to The Inn Way 'pub signs' outside every pub, or ask for the landlord's signature.

Be warned - all the 'clippers' are different!

Send your completed Log Book to the address below to receive your free 'Inn Way Certificate' (please include a SAE as well as your name and address, we will return this Log Book with your certificate). Photocopies of this Log Book will not be accepted.

If you would like to purchase an 'InnWay Certificate' then please write to us for a copy of 'The Inn Way Merchandise' brochure; *"Drinking in the scenery"* T-shirts, 'Inn Way Certificates' plus much more. . .

InnWay Publications,
PO Box 5975,
Birmingham,
B29 7EZ

LOG BOOK PAGE ONE

Day One   **Clip or sign here**

1. Black Horse Hotel, Grassington . . . .

2. Devonshire Hotel, Grassington . . . .

3. Foresters Arms, Grassington   . . . .

4. Tennant Arms, Kilnsey   . . . .

5. Falcon Inn, Arncliffe   . . . .

6. Queens Arms, Litton   . . . .

7. Buck Inn, Buckden   . . . .

Day Two

8. White Lion, Cray   . . . .

9. Rose and Crown, Bainbridge   . . . .

10. Victoria Arms, Worton   . . . .

11. King's Arms Hotel, Askrigg   . . . .

12. Crown Inn, Askrigg   . . . .

Day Three

13. King's Head, Gunnerside   . . . .

14. Black Bull Hotel, Reeth   . . . .

15. King's Arms, Reeth   . . . .

16. Buck Hotel, Reeth   . . . .

LOG BOOK PAGE TWO

Day Four   **Clip or sign here**

17. Bridge Hotel, Grinton   . . . .

18. Wheatsheaf Hotel, Carperby   . . . .

19. Palmer Flatt Hotel, Aysgarth   . . . .

20. Fox and Hounds, West Burton   . . . .

Day Five

21. Thwaite Arms, Horsehouse   . . . .

22. King's Head, Kettlewell   . . . .

23. Blue Bell, Kettlewell   . . . .

24. Racehorses Hotel, Kettlewell   . . . .

Day Six

25. Clarendon Hotel, Hebden   . . . .

26. Fountaine Inn, Linton   . . . .

✦

Name . . . .

Address . . . .

. . . .

Date completed. . . . .

Don't forget the SAE

Printed by Spectrum Print Tel: 01472 340862